The Strangeness of God

THE STRANGENESS OF GOD

Essays in

Contemporary Theology

by

ELIZABETH TEMPLETON

Arthur James

BOOK PUBLISHERS

© Elizabeth Templeton, 1993

World rights reserved worldwide by the publishers

ARTHUR JAMES LIMITED
One Cranbourne Road
London N10 2BT
Great Britain

First published 1993

British Library Cataloguing-in-Publication Data

Templeton, Elizabeth
The Strangeness of God: Essays in Contemporary Theology
I. Title
230

ISBN 0-85305-296-4

Cover Design by
The Creative House, Saffron Walden, Essex

Typeset by
Stumptype, London N20 0QG

Printed and bound by
The Guernsey Press, Guernsey, Channel Islands

Dedication

to Douglas,
whose freedom tests my truthfulness

CONTENTS

Foreword

by The Rt Revd D E Jenkins, Bishop of Durham

It is good to have these explorations, meditations and questionings from Elizabeth Templeton. They present and represent a series of engagements with God pursued episodically "from within". I nearly wrote "they present a series of engagements with *the idea* of God", but that would be an inaccurate and misleading characterisation of the pieces which follow. Of course, if one does not believe in God then these writings must be about "the idea of God" or, indeed, if one is the sort of Christian believer in God who supposes that "theology" must concern discussions about concepts and doctrines to do with God, then, again, one might hold that this book must be a collection of occasional essays about "the idea of God". As Elizabeth herself says, she is setting out attempts at "unacademic theology".

Yet her writing is not about "ideas of God". It is an expression of a series of engagements with God. We have here what I think must be called, in an old-fashioned use of the term, "spiritual writing". For her faith in, and personal experience of, the God of the Bible and of the Christian Tradition, is, quite simply and directly, taken for granted. She is writing out of what has so far been given to her within Christian Church and Christian Tradition. So she is unashamedly and unfearfully writing about God — not for discursive reasons, or for apologetic reasons, or for explanatory reasons — but for exploratory reasons, for reasons of enjoyment and wonder, and for sheer human depth and hope reasons. We are invited to share her engagement — or, at least, to listen, attend, sympathise and be baffled by it (or even sometimes, perhaps, be put off by it) as best we may, for God is there to be engaged with.

The writing is "from within" in several inter-acting ways. Its context, as I have already said, lies very much within Christian Faith, taken for granted and pursued. It comes from within the routine of basic human experiences of family life and love and of their problems. It finds voice from within experienced problems and challenges of how to speak of an unnameable God, and how to be freed from our past; it considers the impossibility and necessity of the Church and contemporary confusions about sexuality. All these realities are lived with and explored from within. I would also venture to say that the writing is about an experience of God within, combined with an experience of, somehow, "being within God" for engagement with God is both the substance and the form of the writings and also their aim.

I hope that many people will come across this book and will persevere in reading it, even when — or perhaps especially when — they do not immediately take to it or, at first, make much sense of it. For I believe there is abundant and increasing evidence across all our societies, not so much of a revival of religious questions (much religious revival is very threatening, sectarian and divisive) but of a revival in the question of, and the quest for, God (even if the symptomatic admission or cry is that we need God to exist but he does not).

Believers must surely respond to this increasing cry and search by just the type of unfearful, taken for granted but entirely open, engagement with God in each and every human question as it is encountered, which is instanced and worked at in the pieces in this book. Selling dogmatisms, moralisms, or sectarian certainties will get us nowhere. People are too disillusioned with religion. The God implied by all too much religious practice and utterance has been discredited by modern insights as simply incredible — and too often undesirable. Besides, God is far too great a Mystery and a Glory for dogmatisms, moralisms and sectarian certainties.

I would hazard a strong hunch that the type of "doing theology from within" which is confidently, while stumblingly and with great openness, exemplified in these pieces is vital to the needs of our times in relation to the God of Glory, Hiddenness and Grace, who is encountered at the heart of the biblical tradition and in the body, person, death and resurrection of Jesus.

This book could well be an invitation, a support, a provocation and a source of hope to many of us; particularly those among us baffled by the impossibility of believing in God, or frustrated by the inability of sharing faith in God or of taking the pilgrimage of our own faith very much further.

David Dunelm
Easter 1993

Preface

"A way of writing a book on the cheap," said a friend, casually about someone else who was doing it, not knowing that I blushed inwardly. Collections of essays, he meant.

It is and it isn't. Clearly the energy, concentration, spaciousness of thought and competence in research which go into a book entered on with planning aforethought is different. This is an attempt to see whether fragments of thinking done over some fifteen years, and mostly since I stopped being 'an academic', have any coherence. It has felt to me like an ongoing exploration, searching and scrutinising in the new context of marriage and mothering whether what I was beginning to think about God was thinkable. That has not, of course, been my only context, but it has been my primary one and — for all the outrage of my more devoutly feminist friends, and my own recurrent shrillness about the horrors of domesticity — I would not have had it otherwise. Theology which cannot face the basic chaos of existence, exposed in family life with young children, has no authority.

That does not, of course, mean that all theologians must be up to their ears in dirty socks, or even that it helps! I owe immense debts to those who are free to think in more sustained and systematic ways than I am. I envy them with recurrent greeness of eye. Sometimes I even lust for their freedom. But I owe it to Kirsten, Alan and Calum that what I think is screened through a resistant mesh of gritty realism, which refuses to legitimate abstraction, hypocrisy and cant. And I owe it to Douglas that whatever temptations I have in the direction of idealism are detected and challenged by a life of unflinching resistance to saying more than can be said in view of the facts: and to dodging the actualities of existence.

The main line of my theological explorations, in terms of discovering a language which seems to bear the weight of the life I live, and of relating it to major insights of Christian faith, grows out of a running conversation with John Zizioulas, now Metropolitan of Pergamum, who was a theological colleague in the early seventies in Edinburgh. His style of doing theology, his completely undoctrinaire scrutiny of ordinary existence in the light of his understanding of God and his scrutiny of our understanding of God in the light of the joy and pain of being human, have vindicated the confidence that undergirds my ongoing pretensions to do unacademic theology; namely that the only qualification to be a theologian is to be as human as possible, and that the detailed specifications of any theological conversation worth its salt are tested by the bearing they have on that humanness.

I am clear that most of what I write here skirts only the edges of doctrinal forests. What deep woods remain to be explored are unmapped by these small chartings of entry points to what I hope is the mystery of God. In defence of their publication, my best response is that I was asked for them by a too generous publisher. If they give anyone else the confidence that you can start where you are and do theology, they may be worth the paper on which they are printed. But as my ecological daughter would remind me, you have to be a pretty awful person these days to abuse this much of a rain-forest!

Since many of the essays started life as occasional papers, they have a lumpiness of context and texture unbefitting to a smooth book. My rationalisation is that it may sometimes be worth showing the working out of a specific demand, since the challenge of where the question comes from seems to be integral to the 'answer'. But, of course, 'Question-and-Answer' seems the wrong model. It is more that you discover what the question is as you interrogate answers. Or you get the sense that this is a big wood when you have had no bother entering it at fifteen different points many days' journey from one another.

In a sense, the first batch of essays is head-on confrontation with themes normally classified as 'Doctrine', and the second batch is with themes often categorised as 'Ethics' or 'Ecclesiology'. Similarly, the forms vary considerably, since the origins of the pieces were for hugely diverse contexts of church, university, locality, and for designated participation in other people's wider agendas. This clearly produces all the raggedness of occasional writing, even where I have tried to eliminate alienating particularities. It is, however, my conviction that the boundaries normally erected between study and pulpit, insider and outsider, specialist and non-specialist are more often to do with the maintaining of empires than with the exploration of truth. My conviction that we are all made for truth, capable of the pain and delicacy of it, able to wrestle for it with both brain and gut is not, I believe, utopian. But we are sadly out of practice at it as a culture in Britain and, even more sadly, in the sub-culture of the churches. The manifest unfinality of these irregular sorties into theological utterance will, I hope, tantalise others into doing better. Any integrity there is in them comes from the confidence others have given me that being free and being truthful hang together.

Elizabeth Templeton
April, 1993

I

Story

Once upon a time, in the time before time began, God said to himself: "I will make something. I do not want it to be made out of myself, for then it would really be me again. I will make something that is itself; something other than me; something quite new; something free; something able to love freely".

So through the creative potency of his freedom, by the brooding of his spirit, he loved the earth into being, and made it out of nothing. And because it was made out of nothing, it was fragile.

Now God loved the cosmos he had made, and said to himself: "How shall I safeguard this frail cosmos, which can so easily fall back into nothingness? I know it cannot live unless it relates to me who can sustain it by my love. But I cannot love it unless it is free, for you cannot love something you make a prisoner of your love. I will not *force* it to relate to me. How can it be that it might love me in freedom rather than out of need or habit? How shall I win its safety without bullying, without snatching it into my safe grasp, without compelling worship?".

And God said to himself: "I know what I will do. I will trust the earth to a creature who belongs to it but is free, whose name shall be man-and-woman. I will make them the gardeners of this cosmos of mine, which cannot sustain itself, since it hangs precariously on the edge of nothing. This man and this woman will steward creation, in the freedom of their being. In love of creation and in trust of me, they will offer it to me to keep alive and whole. I will trust them".

And a voice, the voice of the history that was to be, said: "But God, is that not a bit stupid, a high risk? I mean, would it not be safer just to have a direct power-supply of life to

1

the whole of creation, which was turned on or off by *your* decision, not by the choice of this puny little creature, man-and-woman?''.

And God was angry, and said to the voice of history: "Of course it would be safe; but it would not be love. I will give my creation its freedom, so that its loving of me may not be forced. I could make it so that it turned to me by inbuilt instinct, like a heliotrope to the sun. But I will not do that. For I wish to *invite* it to enjoy my love and share my life, not to compel it".

Then the voice of history said: "But, Lord God, you're stupid. You're over-sensitive about this freedom business. If you give them that much rope, they may hang themselves. At least *appear* to them first in the commanding fulness of your power and beauty, so that they cannot help seeing you and admiring you. Otherwise you may lose them!".

But God said to the voice of history: "Dazzling them into submission is still not trusting their freedom. I will not force them even to recognise me. I will be present-in-absence. I will go away and leave the world as it would be without me, on the edge of nothingness and disintegration: and I will see if the man and the woman have any desire for my being-there, and for the sustaining of creation".

So God went away and left the woman and the man in charge of his earth. And so that he would not dazzle them into worship, he hid the fulness of his beauty from them; and the earth knew death and disease and decay; and was subject to the limits of space and time and cause and effect, and God was present to the earth as a significant absence: as the possibility of love not mapped out with exclusion-zones; as the possibility of freedom stronger than the necessities of cause and effect. And only the imagination of love could see him.

Now the man and the woman lived in the earth as it was. And in their imagination they heard the voice of the significantly-absent God. They heard him say: "Here I am, my people, to whom I trust my earth. You see how it is with you, things are dying all around. People are hating one another and destroying one another. The earth is in the grip of natural necessity. Will you stand with it in solidarity, and offer it to me gladly, so that its pain and fragility may be transformed? If so, I will make all things new".

And the man and the woman looked at each other and said: "Stand in solidarity with the pain! Make all things new! Don't like the sound of that. Of course, eternal life for us would be splendid. But *all things* new! We wouldn't know where we were. After all, as it is, we've got things taped: it's a bit of a bore, all this dying, but you get used to it, and at least it's predictable. We've got the whole earth named and classified; we know who's superior and who's inferior; we know who's normal and who's abnormal, who's reliable and who's unreliable, whom we want to live beside and whom we don't. I think we'll just settle for the limits, thank you very much God, since we are pretty nearly masters of the universe as it stands, with all our intelligence and skill, which will get us by most of the time. This 'all things new' stuff sounds a bit too disturbing".

So the man and the woman kept nourishing each other on the confidence that they had it taped, eating the fruit of the knowledge of good and evil. And the earth stayed in the grip of death.

But God's love was not exhausted: "I know," he said to himself, "I will go to them *incognito*, taking flesh and blood to myself. I who am God will become man-and-woman also. I will invite them as fellow-creatures to offer the earth to my love, and let them see what that would mean. Still, I must be careful not to dazzle them. I will be mistakable for anybody, for nobody. I will take the weight of their hostility to my new future. And I will wrestle with them for the earth, not as God-above but as fellow-man-and-woman".

And God, the meaning and hope of all creation, seeded himself in the depth of flesh and blood in the person of the man Jesus; and held out to the earth from inside the possibility of making all things new. He challenged the classification of his brothers and sisters into normal and abnormal, desirable and undesirable, holy and unholy. He challenged the stranglehold of causal necessity, the limitations of space and time, the right of death to eat the earth, nibbling at it with disease and crunching it with enmity. And so he earthed the possibility of offering everything back to the healing of the significantly-absent God.

But the man and woman were offended. "Who is this," they asked, "robbing us of our right to name things and have dominion over them? He upsets our law and our ethics and even our science. The man is a menace. Let us get rid of him!".

And the voice of history said again: "God, the risk is too great. If you give him into their power, they will win. Protect him. Save him from the danger of his death".

And God said, "No, I will not do that. For unless I go, in my love, to the deepest point of their lovelessness, I cannot reclaim that territory for my invitation to newness. So I will go even there, into the pain of their death".

And the scribes and the pharisees, who were the spokesmen of the man and the woman, and the man and the woman crucified the man who wanted to make all things new.

And the voice of history said, "I told you so!".

But a strange thing happened.

In the community of those who had learned to love this man more than they feared him, the presence of the man who was dead and gone became more alive and potent and convincing than it had been even in his lifetime. It was as if his life too had seeded itself as he surrendered it in the solidarity of being human; and was pushing through the crust of death and hate which seemed to cover the earth, to reappear in new, but recognisable, form.

And in that form again, the absent God became present, and the possibility of new life beckoned the earth.

Those who welcomed the beckoning and lived out of it came

to be called 'church', and knew themselves called to live in the spirit of this Christ who trusted himself and the earth to the spirit of God's future. And they stumblingly bore witness to that, and sometimes tasted its glory.

But the voice of history said: "It's all a con-trick, this story. The dying doesn't stop, and things are not made new. What then is this power of resurrection? Where is the new creation? Why don't you show yourself as Lord of history, if that's what you are? Why doesn't your church stop the dying?".

And God said to the voice of history, "Be patient with me. Enter my patience. I will still not force them to believe. I will wait till the desire of the church for newness in love becomes the desire of the whole earth: and then I will be ready to show myself".

And the voice of history exploded in frustration. "But who can think this will ever be - that the whole earth will desire renewal? Even the church is faithless, sharing the lust of the man and the woman for power, running Inquisitions, shutting out the poor, judging sinners, strutting around in its insider-knowledge of God, damning the rest of the world".

But God said, "Because I love you, I believe in you, history of my creation. I believe in my church, for all its betrayal. I believe in my world, that it can be courted into longing and delight for my future. And till then, I am with you in the suffering, which is the birth-pain of my new creation. I do not sit calmly above it, dusting my omnipotence. Will you wait for me, as the church nourishes this little plant of new possibility which has been seeded for the whole earth? Will you stand by me? Or will you carve out your own way to manage and ward off the world's pain, and leave the rest unhealed in the rawness of death?".

And the voice of history was silent . . .

II

The strangeness of being human

Several years ago, in a series called *Life on Earth*, David Attenborough traced the lines of our evolution from the first primitive cosmic soup to the present day complexity of the natural world.

Religious people have sometimes feared the thrust of broadly Darwinian accounts of creation as being reductionist, of levelling them to merely more complex products of natural selection, 'nothing-more-than' beings, ultimately predictable and explicable in terms of chance and the necessity of survival. Much of the history of European anthropology, at least, has been preoccupied with identifying and attempting to define what *distinguishes* human beings from all other species. Many candidates have emerged: rationality, morality, free-will, responsibility, the capacity for worship. For the greater part of two thousand years, perhaps the most common idiom of expressing the 'difference' has been that of 'soul', a category originating in Platonic Idealism, but massively re-inforced by mainstream trends in Christianity. Variations about the character of souls - whether they were created or uncreated, restricted on a one-to-one ratio to bodies or capable of transmigration, naturally immortal or capable of death - have all been explored, but for many centuries, even when it had long been clear that neither camera nor scalpel could detect this 'soul' as an empirical bit, the term has been a vehicle for the conviction that human beings are somehow *significantly* different.

Interestingly, in Attenborough's last programme he raised the question as to what, if anything, made man unique or distinctive among the multiple forms of life on earth. He asked it, not as a matter of having-to-be-defended dogma, nor as a matter of having-to-be-debunked mythology, but as a sober, curious, empirical question. He made absolutely no reference to the concept of 'soul', perhaps an indication of how thoroughly marginalised now that European Christian consensus is for the intelligent secular world. He resisted, of course, any facile human superiority about rationality, sociability or even quasi-ethical characteristics like loyalty or courage. He, who had documented in breathtaking detail the social and architectural intricacy of an ant-colony, the communication codes of birds, the preservation strategies of desert creatures, was not going to allow any cheap put-down of the way other animals cope with the complexities of their environment.

Nevertheless, his conclusion, as a matter of empirical investigation, was that there seemed to be two things which humans beings did which other animals did not do. One was to laugh, to have a sense of humour. And the other was to use symbols, to *represent* the world.

Animals of course are capable of happiness, contentment, pleasure, game-playing, perhaps even teasing. But the possibility of sharing a joke seemed to Attenborough something which went beyond the possibilities of other species. Nor did it depend on human linguistic sophistication. One of the key episodes in his narrative was an account of how he had been the first white man to encounter a tribe of hitherto unreached forest people in Borneo. Their first meeting, where no common language was possible but only gesture, nevertheless involved a moment where smiles flashed between the two groups at something funny which happened and shared laughter broke out.

The second element also seemed to him distinctively different from the various signals and indicators possible to animals: leaving scent warnings, marking territory, courting rituals, etc. It was the possibility of saying not "I am here, have been here, make this signal", but of using media of communication which did not depend on physical proximity or presence; words which could span centuries and vast cultural spaces; paintings which could give us immediate access to the life of prehistoric people with whom we had no possibility of other physical liaison.

There are, of course, different responses possible to Attenborough's suggestion that these, or any other activities, are distinctively and characteristically human. Two in particular are recurrent polar reactions, both identifiable in the late 20th century.

One is to say "So what?. The distinctiveness is illusory. There may be *quantitative* differences in complexity and sophistication, given the neural apparatus human beings have compared to that of chipmunks and dolphins. But to posit any *qualitative* differences is to project a 'man-of-the-gaps'. More probably, as time goes on, we will discover more and more clusters of other animal behaviour which approximate to representation. Or we will have a less exalted view of human art as we discover its origins in the primitive need of the community to manage the environment or to achieve various strategic ends, no different in *principle* from bower birds choosing blue materials to decorate their nests, or troops of monkeys letting off steam in play. This quest for distinctiveness is itself the sign of an immodest projection, an arrogant dissociation from the rest of the natural world which has rationalised and sanctioned, in the past, all kinds of ecological abuse, cruelty to animals, assumptions of 'lordship' over other living creatures. The recovery of the world's integrity demands our willingness to renounce this dissociative stance, to see ourselves as part of nature, bound up with it as part of an undifferentiated whole of fragile, vulnerable and mutually sustaining interest. People are merely complex animals in a complex environment".

The other pole says, as much of the youth counter-culture is saying, "You see, we told you so. You with your mechanistic rationalist assumption! Nothing reduces to mere material. The world is pervaded by spirit, which we share with the soil and with cabbages and 'humbler' animal species.

"The sterile Christian West with its rationalistic elevation of mind is the problem. Real wisdom is holistic, like Hinduism or New Age Thinking, inviting us to recognise the pervasiveness of these intangibles which have hitherto been monopolised by men. Soul is everywhere. We are all equal in the omni-distribution of life's essential force, the most complex primate and the simplest blade of grass. Any human sense of superiority is not only an illusion, but an evil threat to the balance and stability of the cosmos. We must renounce it as we have painfully learned to renounce the political imperialisms of our past. All life is sacred and soulful."

In both cases, any distance between human beings and the rest of the world allegedly closes, either because we are knocked off any pedestal on which we may think we are, or because the rest of nature is elevated to a sacral status which is identical with ours.

It has become almost a cliché of the environmentally-conscious West that one ideological root of our development into an industrial-technological society with all its attendant ills has been its Judaeo-Christian origins, the Genesis warrant to have lordship over the earth and subdue it, and the 'dominion' mentality engendered by that.

While the abuses which lie on the conscience of Western Europe need acknowledgement and if possible atonement, there is, I believe, another way of mapping the strangeness of being human which takes the distinctiveness of it seriously, without implying any supercilious dissociation. Indeed, it would be a curious irony if, in an act of intended contrition, Christianity renounced its recognition of something which secular anthropology was attending to with interest!

For this capacity for symbol-using, for representing the world, for transcending what happens to be the case in fiction, image or fantasy, and for communicating that transcendence, is a highly significant one. It may, perhaps, serve as a starting point for an exploration which becomes theology if taken far enough — a theology which does not begin by saying "Receive this dogma", but by saying "Explore the implications of your shared existence. Notice that. Pay attention to what is significant".

In this context, it may be worth trying to articulate in terms which become recognisable as theological, what may be at stake around David Attenborough's undoctrinaire observations.

Animals are characteristically bound in their environment, and their highest possibilities are of adaptation to the givenness of things which makes their survival surer. They live instinctively, belonging to the cosmos, as far as we can judge, without the possibility of question, manifesting the rich complexities of biological development.

The poet W H Auden, in a chorus from *The Dog Beneath of Skin*, muses on the point:

> Happy the hare at morning, for she cannot read
> The Hunter's waking thoughts. Lucky the leaf
> Unable to predict the fall. Lucky indeed
> The rampant suffering suffocating jelly
> Burgeoning the pools, lapping the grits of the desert.
> Or best of all the mineral stars disintegrating quietly
> into light.
> But what shall men do, who can whistle tunes by
> heart
> Know to the bar when death shall cut him short,
> like the cry of the shearwater?

The painful power of anticipation, of resistance, of distress at the prospect of something not yet present, of mere possibility, of considering alternative worlds, all that is strangely described as 'gift', being so great a source of disturbance, of malaise. Yet one might contend that it is intimately bound up with any distinctive creativity the human race has beyond the genetically programmed ones of survival-instinct, breeding and eliminating competitors.

...e C

Nº 17325

000

-30TT.

RI-NAPOLI

A JET

0338744O633

...del Golfo S.p.A.
☎ 552 55 89 - Direz. 552 07 63

This capacity, according to the Existentialists for instance, is sufficient reason for not defining persons in terms of the continuities of nature. We can make the future be present. We can bring the not-there before us representatively in paint or word. We can rescue what has been from forgottenness, or from the threat of perpetual obscurity, as the sonneteers remind us, who battle with time for the beauty of their loves and save them, poignantly, for centuries ahead.

This ability to generate and suggest alternative worlds is, suggest, a key starting-point for a theological analysis of nce, whether it be a child's saying "This shoe box is phant" or a Lascaux cave painting or even a lie.

ritic and philosopher, George Steiner, has a fascinating led *After Babel* (published by Faber) in which he he multiplicity of natural languages, and tries to since it seems to serve no obvious biological that book, his third chapter is called "Word " and he spends a great deal of it contending ility of falsehood is a positive and significant n freedom, even of human transcendence:

lsity begin, when did man grasp the power to 'alternate' on reality, to 'say otherwise'? e is of course no evidence, no palaeontological trace of the moment or locale of transition — it may have been the most important in the history of the species — from the stimulus-and-response confines of truth to the freedom of fiction. There is experimental evidence, derived from the measurement of fossil skulls, that Neanderthal man, like the newborn child, did not have a vocal apparatus capable of emitting complex speech sounds. Thus it may be that the evolution of conceptual and vocalised 'alternity' came fairly late. It may have induced, and at the same time resulted from, a dynamic interaction between the new functions of unfettered, fictive language and the development of speech areas in the frontal and temporal lobes. There may be correlations between the 'excessive' volume and innervation of the human cortex and man's ability to conceive and state realities 'which are not'. We literally carry inside us, in the organised spaces and involution of the brain, worlds other than the world, and their fabric is preponderantly, though by no means exclusively or uniformly, verbal. The decisive step from ostensive nomination and tautology — if I say that the water-hole is where it is I am, in a sense, stating a tautology — to invention and 'alternity' may also relate to the discovery of tools and to the formation of social modes which that discovery entails. But whatever their bio-sociological origin, the uses of language for 'alternity', for mis-construction, for illusion and play, are the greatest of man's tools so far. With this stick he has reached out of the cage of instinct to touch the boundaries of the universe and of time.

But while persons, through speech and symbol have a way of expressing resistance to how things are, still, they *are* in certain ways: and a great deal of this century's Existentialist philosophy has tried to plot human existence between the givenness of our context and the freedom of our possibilities.

Heidegger's word for the facticity of existence was 'thrownness', finding yourself launched in an existence you did not ask for, in a specific time and set of relations which you had no part in choosing. There seems no cosmic necessity about your being-there-in-the-world. It just happens to be so. And the sheer contingency of it provokes in us the teasing question "Why is there something and not nothing?", "Why is there me and not no-me?".

This contingency, however, is not merely passively encountered as a *fait accompli*, for we not only exist in thrownness but as possibility. We are not fixed and complete in our being, not simply unwinding with the necessity of a coiled spring or blossoming like a plant specimen. We have, at least to some extent, the making of ourselves, the responsibility of our future. We are charged with care for who we become. The question of "Who will I be tomorrow?" is not simply an enquiry. It is a decision. We are burdened, as no other creature seems to be, by life options.

And yet the options have a fixed parameter, for all our possibilities are in the shadow of death. We are, from our birth, dying beings, and our contingency is marked as clearly by our ending as by our beginning. It is in the face of our sure death that we have to ask who we are, who we will be.

For Existentialism, *the* characteristic human dilemma is whether to face the question truthfully, or to take one of the many ways there are of evading it. One can, for instance, so immerse oneself in business that one never lets it be raised until, of course, a colleague at the next desk collapses over his lunch-time soup. Or one may formally admit it as an issue, but see its settlement as an inevitable process. Death is routine, poses no urgency to life, leaves the directions as they were. "I've lived here since my childhood: my roots are here: I can't move anywhere else." "I'm a good son. I must go into the family business". "I'm bound to fail: see what an emotionally deprived childhood I had." "I'm a Scot. You don't get Scots showing their feelings."

Any kind of unquestioning assumption of a role, particularly one defined for one by others: any collectivism in which I am willing to have myself exhaustively defined in terms of a class's behaviour standards: any determinism which I regard as fixing me absolutely: such acts of 'bad faith' are to the Existentialist the marks of 'fallenness'. For this is, in the eyes of most such philosophers, a world with a tendency towards inauthenticity, pressurising people out of genuine selfhood towards conventional being. As Sartre says in *Being and Nothingness*, "a grocer who dreams is offensive to the buyer, because such a grocer is not wholly a grocer. Society demands that he limit himself to his function as a grocer''. To admit that the sting of death forces us to real grappling as to what we will do with life demands real courage: a basic human challenge in Existentialist eyes, but too rarely met.

It is not that the past must necessarily be renounced, as caricatures of Existentialism sometimes suggest. It may, of course, be positively affirmed. The point is that an active stance must be taken in relation to it: one must not just slide into a ready-made slot. And the dangers of simply letting oneself be conditioned into given forms of being are so great in relation to the past that, for most Existentialists, the future presents a better visual aid to what 'becoming a self' is about. The act of responsibility involved in 'taking a grip' on one's selfhood is clearer when no possibilities are ready-made.

There are other caricatures of Existentialism, sometimes warranted by some of the statements such philosophers have made, which suggest that by will-power a person can do anything from defeating the common cold to renouncing an entire past. This absurdly unrealistic notion in view of our common experience of insuperable physical distress, is one in which the 'real self' is utterly detached from the concrete material world is which it lives, and from the external facts of its history. To recommend that theology reconnects with existence, does not mean dreaming up a *theory* of existence which may in its way be as doctrinaire and arbitrary as other philosophical systems. It means asking whether there are any common conditions of existence which characterise it *as such*, whatever the cultural or sociological differences.

Now that is so big a question that it seems virtually impossible to know where to start. ''How life is'' is how all the novelists and dramatists in the world portray its quirks and particularities. It is how we find the raggedness of our day-to-day activity. It is how the economists and the politicians and the psychologists and the sociologists say it is. It is how fishermen find it — and mothers, and children, and imbeciles, and the very old. It is how the news bulletins report it. It is so complex and elusive as effectively to exclude definition.

We may however bid at identifying a skeleton which, however fleshed out it is in concrete distinctiveness, nevertheless forms the underlying structure of our existence. For if this is not possible, certainly theology fails as a world-embracing world of disclosure.

In the first place we exist within the limits of space-time. The co-ordinates of space and time are for all of us, as for all things, apparently constitutive of our identity. I am a twentieth century British-born version of *homo-sapiens* which has taken a certain form in the world for a certain length of time. That fact also isolates me to some extent. I am incapable of direct communion with, say, a person in Tokyo, or with my great-great-grandfather. If two people I love need me, and they live in different places, I have to decide between them. I cannot be with both at once. I am embedded in a spatio-temporal territory, limited by it.

Secondly, there are limits about which I can do nothing, or at least very little, in my psycho-somatic constitution. I fall asleep, I wear out, I can only cope psychically with so much of certain people. And this is true even when I am, so to speak, at my moral best. It is not an ethical limit, but an ontological one. Nerve-ends and muscle can only stand so much.

Thirdly, there are limits which I face because of the very structure of moral alternatives and choices which arise from these physical limits. Given the world's finite resources, and the vulnerabilities of flesh and blood, I find that my existence is at the expense of others. As a white, twentieth century Britisher, I live off a lot of people in the two-thirds world, killing them slowly by ongoing economic attrition. My taxes go into a defence budget liable to be used against people I do not hate, who will be killed by weapons I deplore. My education and my present opportunities are available to me because money was made available for cleverish children which was not spent on backward starters in the same primary school

15

class. The resources of energy we are now using mean that our great-great-grandchildren will have less. It is not a world where all can have as much as would make us happy or even secure in our existence.

None of these are things I have consciously or individually chosen, but they are facts which involve me: and if I set about altering them, I face other dilemmas. If I cannot help being a white, British, twentieth century, middle-class intellectual, what if I at least "act out of character"? Suppose I stop paying taxes, or I become socially or politically disruptive, either by quiet subversion or overt revolution? I am still faced with questions about how to relate to those I oppose; with the sense that my policies challenge the life-style of others to the point of incompatibility; with problems about where to draw lines and set limits. There is a whole galaxy of people who cannot live with my choices: existentially, that is to say, I have created new enemies. What will I do about them? Eliminate them if I can? Suppress them? Tolerate them? Welcome them? The former two mean that I menace their existence and freedom, the latter two probably that they menace mine. By acting against the standard conventions of my family, my tribe, my race, my class, my peers I am bound to alienate or distress or come into conflict with someone. And by accepting their 'world', I am already surreptitiously alienating others.

Similarly we are caught in all sorts of common dilemmas which are characteristically agonising. I want to speak the truth, yet if I do it in situation X, I will certainly make life significantly harder for my friend Y, who is already under considerable pressure. I want to endorse maximum freedom of speech: but if I do that, my neighbour will spread his poisonous racist policies. Over and over again, what the moral philosophers classify as justice, truth, freedom, love, clash with one another, or generate frightening ironies, whether in the individual or the socio-political realm.

This means that we have to identify ourselves, if we look at our embeddedness in all the natural, social and political contexts of our environment, as beings who are subject to all kinds of fragmentation and erosion. We cannot sustain ourselves against these encroachments: and defences put up against them are liable to be at worst illusory, and at best ironically short-term.

Above all we clearly do not have freedom to enact what we can imagine, a sustainable occasionally longed-for community in which we could be with and for one another in unlimited mutual openness and involvement, unmenaced by any sense of one another's existence as threat. Such freedom, even if acknowledged as imaginatively desirable (and to many it is imaginative nightmare!) is manifestly so impossible as to seem irresponsible fantasy.

The Existentialists, therefore, on the whole, stop at the challenge that we should *choose* authentically. Freedom is choosing, making the future, commitment in one direction. Consequences are less important, even if tragic: and the frustrations and dilemmas which confront us as choosers are part of the demand that we *indeed* choose.

This account, however, seems to pay too high a price for its affirmation of freedom. For, in the end, it invites a kind of dissociation from nature, our own or the world's, which leaves the 'self' attenuated into effectively disembodied will. This, in a fairly subtle way, is a kind of twentieth century Gnosticism, a will to be detached from troublesome flesh, to be pure spirit. But any anthropology which is to do justice to our human identity surely has to avoid discarnation. The form of our being, the looks of eyes, the sounds of voices, the fragility of bones, the location we have in culture, in geography, in history are not accidental to us. They are part of our intimate identity.

Unless these things can also inherit freedom, freedom from dissolution, annihilation, decay, the affirmation that 'we' are free is fantastic.

It is at this point that the representation of the world in art becomes so significant: for it is a paradigm of the human

17

struggle to invite the natural world also into freedom from its own transience; its own 'thrownness' towards death; its own inflexibilities of restriction. Of course, the enterprise is ironic, since the transformed matter which makes the new world — painting, sculpture, film, printed page — is itself liable to subsequent dissolution. Art is not, alas, immortal.

It is, however, a grappling for freedom which involves the stuff of the world, binding 'maker' and world in a new symbiosis of creative mutuality, which is irreplaceably specific and needs both.

There are, of course, many other paradigms of resistance to the way things are — anger, political protest, experiments in alternative life-style, dream. There are utopian visions, recurrently confounded by the limits of human idealism and the recalcitrant stubbornesses of the world. There are ascetic disciplines, understood at best as freeing the flesh, not as freedom from it.

What is crucial in all of these is, according to the perspective of this essay, that they manifest a desire for freedom which seems not to be part of other animal aspiration: not just the 'call-of-the-wild' freedom — resistance to cages and confinement and traps — but freedom to transform the very basic conditions of existence, the matter of fact horizons of possibility we all encounter. That desire, and the partial capacity to attempt it, is the most significant strangeness of being human which merits our reflective attention.

III

The strangeness of God

The whole history of theology could, I suppose, be charted in terms of the fluctuation in people's confidence that God can be 'spoken of'. Some have seen God in obvious continuity with humanity, and described 'him' in unabashedly anthropomorphic terms. As Xenophanes puts it:

> Ethiopians have gods with snub noses and black hair
> Thracians have gods with grey eyes and red hair

Others have so felt the weight of the strangeness of God that they have been reduced to virtual speechlessness, able to say only that God is unlike us in all possible ways, or 'wholly other', and the rest must be silence. (Sometimes, however, the silence is deafening!)

As part of this chequered history, the twentieth century has its own variables ranging, say, from the massive *Dogmatics* of Karl Barth (with their intended obedience to the self-disclosure of a self-vindicating Trinitarian God) to the 'Death of God' theologies after Auschwitz, or Don Cupitt's account of transcendence as a shared fiction by which we construct and fabricate our own meanings, purposes and values.

It is not the purpose of this essay to explore the apologetics issue as to whether God exists. Nor will I argue the pros and cons of one account rather than another of God's self-disclosure.* I remain convinced that there is no conclusively rational vindication of either belief or disbelief in God. That is not to say that *nothing* can be said in the defence of believing. But none of the defences remotely amount to public proof. The ambivalence of faith, even when one is inside it and not

---

* My position on the former question is explored in *The Nature of Belief*, Sheldon Press, 1976

agnostic, seems one of the inescapable burdens of twentieth century, post-Freudian, post-Marxist, post-modernist consciousness. The starting point for this essay is, so to speak, enlarging on the map-reference of classical Trinitarian theology, not trying to plot it or validate its position on the cosmic map by appeal to external authority, but exploring its capacity to generate, sustain and encompass the strange longing for freedom articulated in the previous essay.

Through all the quiet undemonstrative churchmanship of my childhood environment — and the two years of fervent evangelical acceleration in my early teens — nothing really undermined my mental and emotional images of God as a mysterious but recognisably 'bloke-like' person: someone who, for instance, willed, spoke, commanded, was (in the sense of the term which is common in twentieth century English), a personality. This was in spite of clear simultaneous recognition that 'he' did not have the physical correlates and co-ordinates which normally go with being a person, did not occupy space in a way which excluded other things from the same space, had an extraordinary relationship to time in which simultaneity of presence across centuries was possible, and could in no way be pinned down.

To anyone coming at it 'from outside' of course (eg a sceptic or an agnostic) such an account would seem bizarre to the point of incoherence. But as one absorbed the grammar of faith, these things seem 'normal' for God: that he should not be restricted by the parameters of space or time; that he should be able to communicate; that he should have the capacity to override the normal restrictions of nature. There were, of course, dilemmas about *identifying* the voice of God, for instance — to do with how one interpreted scripture or wrestled with one's conscience. But the frame of reference was in principle intelligible and 'livable in'. One had learned obliquely through all the suggestiveness of worship and regular preaching to adjust imagination, language and the expectation involved in calling God 'a person'; to filter out some expectations and retain others.

It was only, for me, with the move into undergraduate philosophy that the deepest challenge about the intelligibility of the whole idea of God voiced itself audibly. Admittedly, the presuppositions behind the questions tended to be empiricist, even positivist, when criteria of verification or falsification were asked for. But the questions themselves were neither inept nor unworthy. Given the diversity of truth-claims made about God in the world of faiths, how on earth did one settle any of them? Was a self-sufficient, self-originating, eternal being not a contradiction in terms? How could it possibly also be designated 'person' when *all* our instances of personal life were bound up with bodies, brains and spatio-temporal co-ordinates? Were all the claims to recognise the will of God not insuperably subjective, and therefore incapable of public vindication? Was it not easier to believe that these systems of mentally staggering assertion grew entirely out of human desire, fantasy, need, and were constructs or projections from them, rather than to explain how they manifested any correspondence with reality?

'Doing theology' in a desperate bid to deal with these subversive questions made the issues a trifle more sophisticated, but not in principle less distressing. One learned, for instance, that the 'gap' between the common-sense use of a word like 'person', and the theological use had been well worked over in terms of the doctrine of 'analogy' — ways of saying "Like, but not exactly like", or "As like X as Y is like Z". But nothing removed the sting of the basic challenge: was all this God-talk irresponsible nonsense, or was there any way of *explaining* its intelligibility in common language which did not depend on a prior commitment to its being intelligible? Could faith and unfaith speak to each other, or were they mutually exclusive circles, each locked into a mind-and-language set which the other could not enter? And within the world of faith, did the shared affirmation that there was God add up to anything worth affirming, if there was such vast disagreement as to the nature of this God, of his will for the world and of his ways of relating to it? Could someone — especially Someone who was supposedly rich with the omnipotence of love, and benevolently disposed to creation — not do better in competent self-disclosure than the history of the world-to-date suggested he was doing — especially if the understanding of his nature and purposes was vital to the world's well-being or salvation? Even given all the malevolences and wilful estrangement of which human beings are capable, could God not reveal himself more conclusively?

In many ways it seemed so much stranger that any God could be and not be clearer, than that there should be no God, only multiple 'God-shaped' constructs, emerging from different social contexts, snub-nosed or otherwise. But then, worship was impossible: for who could worship a construct of his own creation, believing or knowing it to be such a construct? And 'religious experience' crumbled into a kind of agnostic suspension in which all the data could be seen bifocally, in terms both of faith and of disbelief.

During all this wrestling I had, of course, been exposed to the formal structure of Christian theology as Trinitarian, but had never actually realised its central implication existentially, namely that the being of God was not to be looked for or explored as a kind of invisible super-ego, a cosmic buddy, a larger than life personality. The legacy of Augustine, Boethius and Descartes in equating person with 'personality' or 'individual' was too strong in my West

European bloodstream.

But the strangeness of God, if the Trinitarian character of that reality is taken seriously, is that the *last* thing God can be is an individual. Far from being the cosmic projection of our microcosmic existence as individuals, God is the one for whom atomic self-sufficiency is an impossibility, since what identifies him is the uncoerced communion of being in which Father, Son and Spirit *are* only in the mutual giving and receiving which sustains each. It is no *option* for God to be Father, without Son and Spirit.*

Many other understandings of God, of course, resist individualising — all forms of pantheism, the Hindu account of Brahman and various derivatives from that. What is significant about the Christian account is that there is within God differentiation and particularity, though not separation; just as there is, between God and cosmos, differentiation which allows the particularity of each to be real and not illusory. The freedom of God-without-world is marked by the unconstrained participation of Father, Son and Spirit in the communion of being which is God's own identity, and leads to his willed involvement in cosmos through the prism of Christological and pneumatological presence.

This, clearly, is stranger than most gods! And yet the particularity of the strangeness is one which gives the clue at to why this God is 'worthy of worship', not just as a projection of our being, but as a significant alternative to it. The standard grounds for worship — that God is the originator of everything, potent beyond all else, holding the power of life and death — are, after all, not sufficient ground for *adoration*, that is for the willing relativising of our lives in the light of God's life. As the anarchists of history have indicated, robust humanness is just as liable to defy as to glorify such a God.

---

* The intricacy and delicacy of this classical Trinitarian understanding is thoroughly discussed in *Being as Communion*, by John Zizioulas, St Vladimir's Seminary Press, 1985.

What makes God worshippable is that, uniquely in him, freedom and communion converge, neither accidentally nor of necessity, but as the unforced expression of who God will be: a being not intact in the isolation of omnipotence, but open to the infinite dynamic exchange of being, which is the implication of being 'in three persons'. For us, who know over and over again the pull into separateness as the gravity force of our lives and often the apparant *sine qua non* of our survival as free 'persons' (until the ironic point where we realise that death and separatedness come to the same thing), it is the free inseparability of God which is amazing, crisis-generating and rescue-offering. For it is that internally 'vulnerable' solidarity, in which Father, Son and Spirit each 'say' "I am not myself without you as other" which offers the distinctively Christian model of wholeness.

For us, characteristically, community tends to disintegrate under the polar pressures towards individualism on the one hand and collectivism on the other. In Anglo-Saxon and West European culture, the normative anthropology which tends to undergird our ethics, our psychiatry, our legal structures, our property-owning and our use of time is an individualist one. People are atoms, units of responsibility, of success and failure, of entitlement, of consciousness, of belief, of well-being. They may, as a matter of optional possibility, choose to relate in various ways, to form families, join clubs, belong to political parties, support certain ethical codes, share property, but these are voluntary activities, not part of the definition of who they are. That they have been born of a mother and a father, embedded in a cultural context which defines many of their axioms and possibilities, dependent on multiple connections within the psychological/sociological/economic/political framework they inhabit, is related to 'background information'.

In other cultures, collectivism is the polar attraction: there is no concept of the individual, except as deviant or deranged. Society is understood as having a momentum and definition which properly determines the status, role and significance of all its members. Space, time, property belong to the communal group, tribe, state, whatever, and are allocated only by corporate decision and ratification. The 'individual' is subservient to the ends and goals of the whole.

To both these structures, graphically documented in our era by *laissez-faire* capitalism on the one hand and totalitarianism on the other, the Christian account of the being of God offers a significant alternative. For the 'persons' of the Trinity are not individuals who 'decide' to come together, nor parts of a whole, subservient to an organism which determines their identity. The dizzying suggestion of the tradition, particularly in its Cappadocian strand, is that it is the constitutive freedom and generosity of the Father not to be 'by himself' which generates a communion of being in which none is himself by himself, yet in freedom, not by constraint. Such a dynamic unity of being is unthinkable to Platonism with its timeless and changeless deity, or to the popular polytheism of a gang of deities who manifest all the competitive hostilities of the human world writ large.

It is also, of course, virtually unthinkable to 'natural reason' (though in his recent Gifford lectures in Edinburgh University, *Professor Raymondo Pannikar argued that there was an endemic Trinitarian character to much of our apprehension). Why on earth go as far as three or stop there? Why would two persons not be enough for communion, or a galaxy of 'persons' better express the pluriformity of freedom in relationship?

On the one hand, it is staggering boldness that the Church has ventured at all into giving an account of the inner life

* *Trinity and Atheism*: The Housing of the Divine in the Contemporary World, 1988-89, not yet published

of God; the tradition of being silenced before the mystery which is the core of all 'apophatic' theology is a salutary check on any doctrinal complacency. On the other hand, the compulsion felt by the fathers of the early centuries to elaborate a doctrine which is not incontrovertibly in the New Testament itself (if one reads Scripture with historical-critical eyes) is manifest.

One reading of that compulsion is that it arose out of the intellectual pressure to rationalise texts which were, according to the hermeneutics of the time, assumed to be compatible with one another. Another is that it was the extraordinary passion for speculative metaphysics which so characterised Hellenistic consciousness. Yet another, currently the orthodoxy in feminist theological circles, is that it was the conscious or unconscious projection onto the heavens of the structures of patriarchal hierarchy and male collusion.

It seems to me that these accounts are anachronistic or forced. While clearly, the tools of historical critical research were not sharpened to current levels until some two centuries ago, it is a striking characteristic of the homilies of the early church that the rationalising of texts in a comprehensive synthesis is of almost no concern to them. They manifest (even within the New Testament) a freedom to play, to invent, to tell new stories, to interpolate, to qualify what they inherit as the 'given text', and later to allegorise, without, apparently, the slightest qualms about this being an illegitimate activity. Their concern to draw germane pastoral or ecclesiological meaning from texts which have nothing to do with such concerns in their original context is breathtaking, but at least suggests a confidence that God lives and invites risk-taking exploration in terms not entirely dependent on the past. It is only with the loss of that confidence that the Church has to identify its authority sources *absolutely* in the past, either in magisterial pronouncement or in Scripture.

That the thrust was 'speculative metaphysical' seems to imply such distance from the Jewish roots of Christian faith that total dissociation would be involved. But the internal evidence of the disputes about the character of truth, or the relation of God to time suggests rather that the axioms of secular Greek metaphysics are consistently challenged rather than assumed within the early church. And that it was the Jewish Messianic conviction about the historicity of God, and the prophetic insistence on his concrete impact on the life of the community which demanded new paradigms, Hellenistically unthinkable.

The feminist account is supported by the eikonography of much medieval Western and later Trinitarian theology, where the hierarchy of Father, Son, Spirit is visible in all kinds of artistic representation, and in the consciousness of much piety, which dreads the Father, shelters in the Son and ignores the Spirit. But it fails to attend to the shift which seems to have occurred between Byzantine and Byzantine-influenced Christian imagery and that of the West. In the former, even the doctrine of monarchism, in the technical sense that the Father is the generator of the Spirit and the begetter of the Son, is not hierarchical.* It is to do with the insistence that the life of God himself is not a 'mere matter of fact': (it so happens to be three: it could have been nine-hundred and ninety!), nor a necessity for God (all gods worth their salt must be Trinitarian!); but is an implication of the freedom of God to exist as dynamic and willingly interdependent communion. The whole point, so to speak, of the personhood of God as collaborative, is that no one 'person' claims that identity is an individual prerogative, but each expresses the mutuality of being which leaves none with a monopoly of existence. This may be articulated, on the whole, in gender pronouns, which

* Zizioulas, op cit, page 44 ff

are masculine, but the subverting of what our Western culture normally means by 'self-sufficiency' is more radical than anything which either patriarchy, matriarchy or egalitarianism have so far produced. It depends on a transformation of existence which does not define itself in terms of rights, but in terms of belonging, and of a belonging which is not identification of nature, but community of freedom.

Against all the tendencies of our experienced existence, that surely invites exploration of the suggestion that it is possible to be, not as a defender of one's *right* to be, but as a witness to one's interdependence on everything else that is around. The generosity of being which *invites* as co-extensive with its own breath the interdependence of others, is to staggeringly strange as to deserve attention. And that attention cannot be neutral. It will either be resistant and hostile, resenting the suggestion that individual being is marked by death, or it will be responsive to the invitation to belong in that context of being which alone can sustain life, where the very structure of being-individual is rejected, and particularity is generated not by separatedness but in relationship.

How does one get into all this? What are the access points? Why should any of it be believed, since it is clearly no more self-evident than any of the alternatives like 'First Cause' or 'Ultimate Source of Value', and no less abstract and intangible?

It is of course the answer of devotion to say that one gets into it 'by grace' or 'by revelation' — responses which at best are pointing out that the presence of God catches one by surprise and not in response to virtue, spiritual technique and so on. That is, however, singularly off-putting to the outsider who says in protest "But then why is it not revealed to me? Why do I not find it credible? Why can I not get behind the acres of words to the convincing reality of this Trinity you affirm? If bumping into a super-bloke was the wrong expectation, how does one bump into the Trinity?''.

Here again, I think the whole framework of expectation needs to be challenged. There may, of course, be 'special religious experiences', visions and the like, moments of particular ecstasy and so on. But they are not, I believe, what 'the experience of God' is about. That is rather, under the conditions of our existence, a more oblique state of affairs, not usually isolable in specific moments.

In one sense, the shorthand answer to where it comes about is 'in the life of the church'; but the shorthand becomes so misleading in the context of our ghettoed ecclesiastical existences that it is probably best avoided. Or, at least, before one ventures into ecclesiology, it might be clearer that one is not moving into claustrophobic anti-world sectarianism polarising Christian and non-Christian.

To clarify that, to suggest that the 'encounter with God' is an intelligible notion but one which is discovered in a suffused way of grappling with our shared humanness, is a slow and painstaking business. It involves some account of the relationship between Christian discourse and certain salient features of our common experience, Christian or not.

For if, as Christian faith claims, the strangeness of God touches the whole of creation, no account of it will do which reduces it to the privileged experience of a clique.

IV

On knowing the unnamed God

In one sense, this will be an exercise in 'natural theology', because it is exploring the realities of common human existence. In another sense, it is theology which has looked up the back of the Christian book, informed not just by neutral rationality or by universal religious sensibility, but by an involvement in precisely Christian traditions.

The question I want to ask is perhaps a crude one. Certainly in many concrete situations it seems either patronising or indelicate to voice it. Yet it seems to me a question which is both intellectually haunting and experientially troubling. It may be framed like this:-

"If I meet people who never name God, or who name him differently from me, or even verbally deny his existence, have I any way of judging whether they know the God I believe I am involved with in Christian faith? Or indeed, if I meet people who affirm the same Christian propositions as I do, can I explain my not uncommon suspicion that, despite a shared vocabulary, we are *not* talking about the same God?"

The question came into focus very sharply for me in 1983 when I went, through the British Council of Churches, with a group of church leaders as guests of the Vatican for a week's conversations. In the course of meeting the whole range of Curia departments and secretariats, we had in particular two encounters which suggested different poles of understanding. At the Congregation for the Doctrine of the Faith, headed by the highly intelligent and articulate Cardinal Ratzinger, a position was argued which, in a curious way, reminded some of us of Protestant scholastic Calvinism. If God has disclosed himself for our salvation, the argument ran, that must entail that he has given us sufficient determinate truth to be expressed in adequate determinate propositions. Truth is not a *goal* to which theological affirmations *approximate*. We are entrusted with a quite sayable, teachable truth. And indeed, participation in the community of faith, in eucharistic sharing and in the very knowledge of God, is properly correlated with willingness to affirm or receive such truths, such namings of God as the church authorises through its magisterium — the defined 'substance of the faith'.

By contrast, a few hours later, talking at the Secretariat for non-Christian religions, where the staff is specifically engaged in dialogue with people of other faiths, the picture was very different. Here it was several times affirmed that people whose assertions were, on the face of it, quite incompatible with received Catholic doctrine, were nevertheless intimately involved in knowing God. Indeed the whole understanding of mission within this department was one of mutual dialogue in which God's truth was given and received by both partners in the conversation. This, of course, provoked a host of questions as to how one identified those aspects of another faith or culture.

On a more domestic scale too, like teaching in a theological Faculty in Edinburgh, or in a church in Birmingham, the problem exists equally clearly. One need not be entirely sceptical about the capacity of our words and sentences as tools for mapping reality: yet one must be sobered by the awareness of how many meanings are liable to be taken from almost any theological utterance one makes. The traditional words of most religions become encrusted with historical accumulations, like barnacles on a ship, and it takes a lot of underwater exploring to find out what layer of meaning any given speaker is associating with a common word. What Irenaeus meant by calling God powerful was not what Calvin meant. What the Israelites meant by calling God judge was not what St Ignatius Loyola meant. What the fifth century

Byzantines meant by naming God as Trinity was not the tritheism which Jews and Muslims often suspect of Christianity. And what *any* learned or unlearned user of God-talk means today by it is liable to be at some variable distance from any usage of the past, and many of the present time.

Most people however, have only the most limited awareness of such layers beneath the religious language of their own context and are often at the mercy of the words they have learned. They innocently import into the words of the past meanings which belong to the present, and assume they were always there. (They hear, for instance, 'God in three persons' and assume a 'person' is an individual psyche.) They are effectively trapped in one particular stratum of religious language, or even in one author's interpretation, and all the associations and resonances of that use attach to the word wherever they read or meet it. Most people inherit their religious vocabulary either unexplained 'by use and wont' or with minimal explanation inside a very defined context.

The grounds for being significantly dismayed about this are not simply that academic injustices are being done, traditions confused, texts misunderstood. They are more human. The tragedy is that if people slip too early into some given religious language, they may *un*learn how to be truthful about what might be called the phenomenology of their own existence. They are taught a religious language which straitjackets their own possibilities, becomes their only acceptable frame of reference and narrows their response to others who do not name God in the same way.

Take, for instance, the case of a small child growing up within earshot of a Christian community. Suppose for the moment you believe, or will entertain the notion, that children, before they can verbalise or conceptualise, already are persons who in some significant sense 'know God'. This supposition is not just a piece of sentimental romanticism, but a gloss on the New Testament suggestion that "of such are the kingdom of heaven". Suppose for the moment it might mean that small children's capacity for love, their directness, unmarred by self-consciousness, their purity of rage, their relativising of the world's social conventions are, somehow, manifestations of their relatedness to God.

As they grow, however, children hear, or overhear, words about God. They gather that God can be talked to, for instance, and wonder how. Perhaps equations are made for them between the voice of God and what is in the Bible, or the voice of God and one's conscience: or between the voice of God and certain psychically distinctive moments of special experience (Samuel, Saul, classic conversion experiences, etc). Gradually, if this is sustained, a child comes virtually to equate the communication of God either with such isolable episodes of somehow abnormal experience or, in a more liberal tradition, with his or her own ethical convictions or again with authoritative pronouncements of some religious authority or text. Once this is done, the possibility of sustaining and cherishing that knowledge of God, which is detectable in the child's very existence, dwindles, sometimes to vanishing point. For as soon as the growing child becomes sceptical about special supernatural experiences or absolute ethical authority, the most irreversible agnosticism about God is liable to set in. The named God is undermined by doubts, and the unnamed God is not recognised.

It is however time that I explained more what I mean by this 'unnamed God' who may be known by the child or the unchurched or even the actively atheist. When I said at the beginning that I had "looked up the back of the Christian book" I meant to dissociate myself, for example, from that school of natural theology which argues for an objectively compelling belief in an infinite first cause, or a ground of moral absolutes. My presupposition in this essay is that the unnamed God, when named, is in fact the Trinitarian God. (It would be a long detour for me to say why I am convinced of this, while recognising the powerful contemporary

33

arguments that the doctrine is a fossilised lump of impossible metaphysics. It would be wrong too, in my view, for the Trinitarian formulation to be accepted *simply* because it is the dominant tradition. I also recognise, living under the same roof as my husband, a New Testament specialist, that there are major exegetical questions about how the doctrine relates to post-critical Biblical scholarship. Nevertheless I work as a theologian with a sense that the details of Trinitarian formulation are all part of a wrestling of which I want to be part, a wrestling to articulate how love and freedom are already endemic in God's own life, so to speak, quite apart from his relations to the subsequent world. In spite of the critical pressures, I still find this the area which clearly distinguishes the Christian God from the ideals and vision of most kinds of natural theism or from the pantheist view of an omnipresent spiritual reality, equidistant from everyone and everything, or from the Esperanto God synthesised out of a course in comparative religion.)

When I say that it is this God who may be known, unnamed, by the child, the unchurched or the atheist, I am not, however, saying that he is bound to be known. It is, of course, a tempting theological axiom that *a priori* we all know God. It avoids the awful theodicy question bound up with the idea of selective election. It challenges the intolerant arrogance which has, in the past, given rise to savage, proselytising heresy hunts, inquisitions and so on. If everyone is assumed to know God, then *God's* generosity is more clearly vindicated, and we are predisposed to a more generous reading of one another's beliefs.

Nevertheless, I think it is vital to go on saying that the unnamed God is not *automatically* known. I have hinted that the distinctive ontology of God in Christian thinking is to do with a mutuality of love and freedom which is uncoercive. It is incoherent to suggest that a God of such a nature would *constrain* response, even epistemological response. If we work with the Semitic undertones of the word to 'know' which inform the early church, knowing anyone is in fact a complex recognition, involving will and feeling as much as mind. We are not passive in knowing, not merely acted upon by the impinging world or the impinging God. However widely God's freedom may intend or invite — and my convictions here are universalist — no one can be *bound* to know him. It would be a subtle return to the God of omnipotent determinism to claim that he commands universal recognition.

My second resistance to the liberal assumption about the universal knowledge of God is more existential, more political if you like. When I heard Mrs Thatcher speaking the prayer of St Francis as her mandate to govern (as she did in addressing the General Assembly of the Church of Scotland), while she cradled the latest torpedo in the ordnance factory: or when I hear someone like Ian Paisley rabble-rousing against the Pope in fanatic Protestant Irish terms: or when yet another Vatican cardinal says divorce is impossible because God's law has nothing to do with human experience, I simply do not believe it is the same God about whom we are all talking. The assumption is too bland to do justice to the critical, divisive, conflict-generating God of prophets and apostles.

Of course, I should be properly checked in my confidence that *I* am the one who knows God, by all sorts of New Testament rebukes — the parable of the wheat and the tares, the repeated irony of self-righteousness confronted by eschatological shock. I am indeed, in one sense, defined as a member of a eucharistic community (loosely understood) which embraces me and Mrs Thatcher and Ian Paisley and Cardinal Knox. But, so help me God, I do not believe that all the various commitments and perceptions of these people are equidistant from God's truth. Some of them seem to me gross violations of faithfulness to the God I think I am in the process of knowing. And I prefer to risk the sifting of God to the bland neutrality of *laissez-faire* non-alignment.

What I need then, when I venture the existential confrontations I find unavoidable, is a working criterion which is sensitive enough to look deeper than the words people say, yet definite enough to distinguish in principle between those who know God and those who do not.

The most obvious and historically accredited candidate is probably what the tradition calls 'the fruits of the Spirit', and more recently liberation theologians identify as *orthopraxis*. That is, where people feed the hungry, clothe the poor, where they manifest gentleness, patience, humility, etc., there one sees the enacted knowledge of God, whatever people say. And where they ignore the poor, neglect the outsider, bully, boast and congratulate themselves on their splendid faithfulness, one sees the enacted absence of such knowledge.

This position certainly has its attractions: it seems to me in a way closest to the actual challenge of the probable historical teaching of Jesus, and it certainly corrects the abstracted concentration on head-knowledge and speech within our religious histories. Nevertheless, even this position seems to me to have two major limitations which, if not fatal to it, at least severely restrict its absoluteness.

First: just as words are highly ambivalent until you can pinpoint context, linguistic tradition, specific usage and so on, so any specific action belongs to a whole world of intention and interpretation. The same act, the same apparent policy may in fact be quite a different thing in two cases. Take, for example, the alleged virtue of chastity, in the minimal sense of abstinence from sexual activity for the unmarried or of sexual monogamy for the married. This may happen out of loyalty, or because one believes that divine sanctions will meet its violation. It may increasingly in our world happen as a symbolic stance against the natural tide of biological instinct or against the ideology of family. The minimal description of sexual continence becomes highly differentiated when put into such contexts. I think it could be argued that most actions are improperly named without such specifications which involve access to all the interiority of need and motive. Orthopraxis can rarely be confident of having that access.

Second — and this is a theologically more central problem — there is a risk in this, which Protestantism has sometimes recognised, of turning the knowledge of God into a self-justifying ethic. We must not equate the community of faith with the aggregate of those robust souls who survive the stresses of existence with confident and discernible ethical self-sufficiency. There is, of course, throughout the New Testament a constant challenge for some kind of correlation between faith and life. Yet there is something as important in the Gospel as the emphasis on transformation. The Lutheran slogan, *simul iustus et peccator*, is no bad summary of it. The achievement of conspicuous sanctity may signal extraordinary closeness to God, but it cannot be made a *criterion* of membership of His kingdom. For the new community consists, for the present time, of men and women being made and remade in the image of God, recurrently failing, but not fixed in their failure. The risk of 'fruits of the Spirit' criteria is that they demand achievement when the reality is much more often a tension between vision and achievement which is precisely generated by the Gospel.

So far then, I have argued it can be neither the believing or not believing of specific propositions, nor the doing or not-doing of specific acts which indicates the knowledge of God. It is, rather, a complex mode both of thinking and dismantling thoughts, of doing and failing to do this or that.

Let me, for the rest of this essay, expand if I can on this complex mode.

The kingdom of God, as signalled in the New Testament, seems to me to be that condition of transformed existence in which men and women participate in the fulness of love and freedom which is God, sharing the quality and scope of love and freedom found in the mutuality of God's own life as Father, Son and Spirit. That freedom is not, in God, a matter of choosing among options, but a way of being that expresses without loss or constraint the fulness of God's self. In that sense it seems to me one of theology's more obvious and damaging anthropomorphisms to interpret freedom in God in terms of choice. God does not have to decide among possibilities, for the gap between possibility and actuality is, for him, non-existent. What he can do he is doing: and there is nothing he could choose to do which he is not doing. This conviction, which lies I think behind the classical Christian understanding of God as *actus purus* is in sharp contrast to the debate in classical natural theology about the omnipotence of God, where dilemmas are set up precisely in terms of divine options, seen as essential to the freedom of God.

If you want reference points in our kind of experience for glimpsing that possibility, I suppose they are the various forms of 'being in love', whether with another person, with an artistic creation, or with a political cause. In some significant sense, existentially, it does not feel as if we choose them. We do not opt to be in love. Yet when we are, we do not feel passive but activated, as if here we were maximally ourselves-with-the-other, able to be in virtue of our relatedness to him/her/it. The analogy will break, of course, if pushed too far. The force of the erotic and the constraint of the domestic cannot be sustained for long without a swoop into caverns of necessity and restriction: yet without sentimentalising or romanticising, I think we may find, in our quite mundane experience, twinges of what it is to be free in the manner of God.

The freedom is, however, unsustainable under the conditions of our existence. Or, more precisely, insofar as it *is* sustained it will put the world in crisis and generate the conditions for lynching. For it is correlated among other things to the absence of various constraints such as death, spatio-temporal limitation and causality which *are* the conditions of our existence. It is an internal debate within Christian theology why such constraints exist but, to anticipate, I place them as belonging not to God's creative intentionality for the world, but to its 'fallenness': its willed distance from God's intention. To insist on the unsustainable freedom as the proper, inviting destiny of human beings is to refuse to settle for the conditions of finite existence, and if that cannot be cashed in terms of precise actions, it can at least be cashed in terms of 'resistance', of refusal to believe that this is what we are made for, what we are called to.

The freedom of God, however, is not at odds with, not out of relation to, God's other defining attribute which is his love. Indeed that being which is fully actualised in the freedom of God is a freedom of belonging-with, of a give-and-take relatedness in which identity is not defined in terms of independence and separateness, but of a particularity which comes through irreplaceability in communion, through mutuality of being, freely interdependent.

At its most general then, the question of whether people know God is, I am arguing, bound up with the question of whether they live in and with the tension generated for existence by the presence, or the significant absence, of such love and freedom. That is not a condition identified or guaranteed by any single act. People may pick up, feel, respond to one particular aspect of the tension and ignore others. They may even fail to recognise their own response as significant. (It is, for example, a common feeling in many people, when they are needed in two situations they care about, to chafe that they cannot be in two places at once. Normally the feeling is not allowed to surface as valid, because people have been taught, religiously, that being in one place is a human being's *proper* state; that the desire for anything else is *hubris*, and that omnipresence is strictly for God. So an intuition of what love-in-freedom means existentially, as simultaneous presence, becomes smothered.)

In other cases, people may register a 'syndrome' of resistances and of preoccupations which indicates the frustration and yearning involved in our natural incapacity for love and freedom, given the structures of the cosmos. The resistance may, interestingly, even be manifested as explicit atheism (if the learned, named God, as in much Western theology, has been a limit to human freedom, it is a tribute to the unnamed God, for example, that modern French existentialism has been conspicuously atheist). Similarly, the named God whom Marx denounced was the one who gave cosmic permission for the isolation of manager from worker, and Marx's political rage was a tribute to the unnamed God who invites us into non-exclusive relationship with one another.

In the vast majority of cases, people are not sophisticated enough to have forged explicit doctrines, and may either belong or not belong in Christian community at quite different levels of their existence. I suspect that the vast majority of human beings have some apprehension or intuition of the unnamed God which they may never allow to put pressure on the received ideology or religious categories they inherit. For instance, it may be only at the point of bereavement that people discover how wrong death is, how it dismantles the world's relationships. For most of the time head, and even heart, reconcile themselves to death as biologically necessary and universal: and common sense and social convenience demand that people carry on managing in the absence of the missing one, safely dead and buried. Only the dogged refusal of the lover to be reconciled to the absence of his love suggests the truth. The world is not 'itself minus one' when someone dies. It is dismantled. For love, the world minus the loved one becomes a non-world, and the incapacity to restore that integrity of creation may even lead to the lover's death as a testimony to the brokenness of things. Even the child, momentarily inconsolable at the loss of a favourite toy catches the quality of it. So does the poet, spitting rage at time and distance and death. One could work out a whole range of characteristic and quite undoctrinaire responses which, from this theological perspective, become responsive intuitions of the unnamed God. This may be quite at odds with the formal response people offer to the named God. Indeed, in our culture, Christianity, God has become so identified as the cause of death, the taker-of-people-to-himself, that the proper

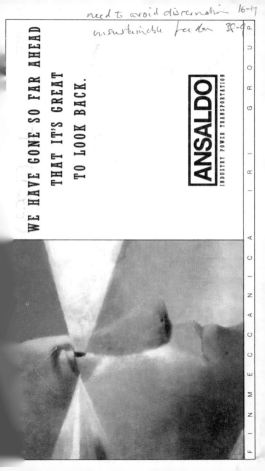

WE HAVE GONE SO FAR AHEAD
THAT IT'S GREAT
TO LOOK BACK.

ANSALDO
INDUSTRY POWER TRANSPORTATION

F I N M E C C A N I C A · I R I · G R O U P

BA2607/030CT RICHARSON/JP

VOLO
FLIGHT

DATA
DATE

NOME PASSEGGERO
PASSENGER'S NAME

DEST
DEST

CLASSE
CLASS

LGW Y

SEAT

POSTO

15F

ASSISTENZE
ASSISTANCES

POSTO NON
FUMATORI
SE BARRATO

NO SMOKING
SEAT WHEN
CROSSED

GESAC

carta d'imbarco
boarding pass

Conservare la carta d'imbarco sino
all'arrivo e non cambiare il posto senza
aver consultato l'assistente di volo.

To be kept until arrival.
Do not change seat without consulting
your cabin attendant.

verbal response might well be rage or atheism.

Again, the tension may be expressed either in tragic or comic modes. At its most painful and black, it may generate such pain as to tip the balance from sanity to insanity. I have one friend at least whose faithful attention to the lovelessness of the world threatens her psychic stability. Yet it may also take wildly comic forms, where it is *humour* that offers resistance to the world's *status quo*. At any rate, there are multiple manifestations of it once you start looking in these terms, refusals to accept, in some sense, the laws of social management, property, money, sexual taboo, political status and so on. This may at any time send people over the edge of what the community defines as 'normality' and so may be counted as dangerous, criminal or deviant. That is why, again with New Testament reverberations, there is a lot to be said for looking for glimpses of the unnamed God among a community's marginals or aliens: the artist, the criminal, the lunatic, the unsocialised child, the hermit may all express, in play, fantasy or alternative perception, a significant protest against the community's named Gods.

Or again, the tension may take socio-political forms, though these can never be equated absolutely with 'the will of God'. Even political resistances, to be effective, have to acknowledge the constraints of causality and the managerial necessity of power structures, whereas God is the antithesis of both. Yet there are political aspirations whose direction seem to me cognate with the kingdom of God; negative ones against existing constraints, and positive ones for the extension of human solidarity. Every refusal to dehumanise the declared enemy is an involvement with the truth of the unnamed God. Any attempt to abolish the boundaries which become pretexts for separateness in our world — race, sex, class, intellect, even forms of religious affiliation — may be seen as commitment to a vision of human inter-identity which has its ground and source in the inter-identity of the Christian God.

The vision may be fragmentary. The Marxist antagonism

to class conflict was voiced in terms of a kind of economic determinism which itself may be seen as a major unfreedom for human beings. It may be distorted by utopianism, as when visionary communities underestimate the power of various interest groups in society, or expect their vision to be socially realisable without costly conflict. One may never be able to 'manage' a community of love and freedom, to live without compromise before the eschalon. But still one may be faithful, in irony, passion or hope to the distance between the manageable and the kingdom of God. There may be analogies in socio-political terms too between the lunatic, the poet and the lover and those who crusade for anti-apartheid, nuclear disarmament or fair trade policies, taking on the world's settled injustice and cruelty. The passion which moves them, the constant frustration is, I suggest, another relation to the unnamed God which is pre-, sub-, or supra-doctrinal.

No one is able, or indeed usually entitled, to assess how in this or that particular person the knowledge of the unnamed God has been corrupted by the learned distortions of culture, theology and piety. How far, for instance, is X's neurosis generated by the contrast between existence and eschatology, and how far is it the product of inculcated fear and guilt about a demonic and punitive God? Occasionally, one may be in such relations of personal or pastoral intimacy with people as to explore the issues in a specific case, but that is a delicate matter, not accessible to outside judgment.

My main point in this essay is to argue for a willingness among theologians and philosophers of religion, and indeed among people of faith or faithful doubt, to go behind the propositions which so often constitute theological argument; and to try to uncover what they take to be existentially at stake in knowing or not knowing God. I think that theology cannot recover freshness, nor the world interpret its own theological dimension, until we look beneath the surface of the words for and against God to the existential allegiances and longings which identify who we are.

V

On undoing the past

This issue, though apparently bizarre, arises directly from the more immediately recognisable problem of evil. For it seems clear that much of what *is* evil in the world — much, that is, which frustrates the convergence of freedom and love in our existence — is rooted in the past and in the fact that we are stuck with it. As Dorothea Solle curtly sums it up in her book *Suffering*:

> The fourteen-year old child Chaim is dead. From which face then shall God wipe away the tears?

It is the platitudinous fact that time does not stand still, that the same water cannot flow twice under a bridge, which faces us with the irreparability of things, whether it takes the passive form of pain at transience or the active one of self-disgust and shame. I am the person who was too young to remember my parents. He is the man who engineered his friend's dismissal. We are the generation born after Hitler. For good or ill, we identify ourselves in relation to our past, time and what it brings being one of the co-ordinates by which we distinguish ourselves from others. Yet sometimes we recognise the menacing fact that this same past which has particularised our existence threatens to define us, heaving barrowloads of 'facticity' into our present out of which we cannot crawl.

The main presupposition of this essay is that unless theology is willing to tackle the question of undoing the past, it can never hope to articulate a theodicy, no matter how rich a present or rosy a future it may hold out. Or, if theodicy seems an impudent venture, it cannot give a convincing account of salvation. For unless Hell, where the prisoners of the past live, can be somehow harrowed, the theological enterprise is dubiously worth it.

What I shall try to do in this essay is less to defend that contention, though it may be the controversial eschatological tail which wags my theological dog, than to investigate what it might mean and what it might not mean to speak of undoing the past. I shall try to do this in ways which avoid doctrinal jargon but I invite tolerance of one technical term, now taken over by the *Penguin Dictionary of Music* from Bishop Irenaeus of Lyons. The term is 'Recapitulation', an image which I find, for reasons to be explained, less intolerable than most for the difference Christ has made to things, or more technically, for the doctrine of Atonement.

I have no wish, however, to be hoist on historico-exegetical petards. It would be rather nice to be batting in the same team as Irenaeus, and I do intend to be interpreting rather than misinterpreting him. But if on investigation you were to conclude that he did not say what I am about to say he said, it is at least sayable! And it is really about that 'sayability' that I would like to provoke thought.

'Undoing the past' is, to common-sense and the average Anglo-Saxon philosopher, nonsense of the type known as self-contradiction. It is virtually analytic or tautologous that the past cannot be undone, a matter about which no debate could be envisaged among those who have learned English in a world where cats either sit, or not, as the case may be, on the mats, and where reality is table-shaped and two plus two make four.

The suggestion that it is theologically necessary to affirm it therefore takes us willy-nilly into another field of contemporary debate, namely the relation between 'theological speech' and 'ordinary language'. At this point I disclose a second presupposition of the essay: that there should be no special pleading for a private theological language whose inner logic is in principle inaccessible to those outside the game. What is at stake is how the world is, and the debate must be as public as existence, both in its vocabulary and in its data. It may of course be that the identification of self-contradiction is less a neutrally axiomatic matter than a verdict related to a whole interpretative mapping of reality. But such maps are, I believe, open both to anyone's scrutiny, and to not-irrational debate.

Even if one can effectively slip the logical cordon, however, and insist that it is intelligible to wish the past undone, one becomes at once an object not of philosophical but of alarmed psychotherapeutic concern. If wanting to undo the past is not impossible, it is at least unhealthy. Thus Henri Ellenberger, in an article (as I recall but cannot trace the French psychological journal) dauntingly entitled "A Clinical Introduction to Psychiatric Phenomenology and Existential Analysis", writes:

> Regarding the mutability of the past, it is our common experience that the past is closed, and cannot be changed . . . However, in certain paranoid patients, the past is highly mutable.

Ellenberger then introduces a phenomenology of time suggested by one Minkowski, in which the remote past is the zone of the obsolete, the mediate past the zone of the regretted, and the immediate past the zone of remorse. Sanity, by common consent, knows this: the milk which is cryable over must have been recently spilt, and not cried over for too long. Battle with the factuality of the past, especially of the past for which we are not responsible, can only be categorised as fantasy, wish-fulfilment or sheer delusion. Maturity, on such an account, is to do with recognising the appropriate responses to the various zones of lived time, adjusting harmoniously to the past. So we have a whole pastoral strategy endorsing the need to reconcile people to what has happened, and even a sinister liturgical ghost stalking funeral parlours, who suggests that everything which has happened must, *ipso facto*, have been in accordance with God's will.

There is, of course, one school of contemporary philosophy which has seen something of the negativity of the past, and it might be supposed that this essay is merely an exercise in post- adolescent Existentialism. Certainly in refusing to accept a determinist account of human identity, existentialists seem sometimes to be suggesting that the past is unreal; that an act of will can enable one to take off and fly in the freedom which the future offers to the present, with no reference to one's rootedness in the past. Accepting the givenness of what has happened, its fixity is a construct of false consciousness, the realm of evil and unreality.

Such a divorce between past and present seems itself both unreal and unhappy if it implies that a person is only his or her future, the past thinning like a vapour trail into oblivion. Such self-estrangement as involves the virtual renunciation or abolition of one's earlier self is too high a price to pay for newness.

On the whole, however, I suspect that only crude caricatures of Existentialism invoke so radical a dislocation. Sartre, for instance, while constantly castigating those who identify themselves *entirely* in terms of their past, with a kind of Classical Greek fatalism, wishes rather to emphasise that it is the *isolation* of the past which is a paradigm of *mauvaise foi*:

> The past cannot be possessed by a present being which remains strictly external to it, as I remain, for example, external to my fountain-pen
>
> (*Being and Nothingness*, p 112,
> ed. Barnes, New York, 1956)

and

> The present is not; it makes itself present in the form of flight . . . Here then we are referred to the future.
>
> (ibid p. 123)

Properly, existentially, he is saying the past is unintelligible without reference to the present, and the present without reference to the future.

But here, precisely, lies our problem. For, ontologically speaking, the future of beings in time is death, whatever psychological revisions of self-understanding we undertake. The future of any concrete thing will be to have been; an image of a kind of cosmic black hole steadily sucking creation into itself, and apparently winning. Mental stoicisms and solipsisms may keep us going through the galloping present *feeling* intact, but if we consider the natural future and the absence of others, we are as ontologically precarious as ever. Certainly, if we wish to affirm that our identity is inextricably bound up with this solid earth, and the specific people with whom we are involved, the strength of our memories and the foreseeable continuation of a world is no comfort. When they die, *they* should be here, and are not, whether or not I am psychically undone by their absence or not. That is the essay's third and most important presupposition, that it is necessary, if love is love, that it should not be reconciled to the loss of any specific being which it loves.

When, in music, a recapitulation takes place, the notes may apparently be identical in their first and second occurrences if, that is to say, one isolates the particular sequence of notes which makes up the theme. But if one hears them relationally, all that has gone before makes the second playing so different from the first that it exerts a kind of retrospective pull. Hearing the recapitulation, you hear what you heard before, but your before-hearing is modified by your after-hearing.

This musical application seems to me a not inept one for glossing Irenaeus on the redemption of time. The before-hearing of the world's nature and history, its Adamic existence, is modified by the after-hearing, the life of Christ. The ground is re-trodden, the territory re-explored, the possibilities of existence re-investigated, and the outcome re-concluded. In the most concise summary statement of *Adversus Haereses*:

> God recapitulated in himself the ancient formation of
> man, that he might kill sin, deprive death of its power
> and vivify man, restoring him to His (ie God's) own
> liberty.

That the notes, so to speak, in the Adam theme and the
Christ recapitulation are truly parallel is a point which
Irenaeus constantly emphasises, occasionally labours, and,
from a twentieth century historical perspective, sometimes
fiddles. For instance, both Adam and Christ were born
without fathers, both with genuine flesh, bone and nerve
identity — the latter not a thing to be taken for granted about
Jesus in the context of Gnostic controversy. Both were in a
sense dependent on the responses of the women in the
respective stories to God's will, Adam conditioned by Eve's
disobedience, Christ by Mary's openness. The fate of the one
was linked to his attitude to a particular tree in Eden, of the
other to a corresponding tree in Golgotha.

Whatever the quaintness of the detailed typology (and I find
it offensive only if it is used as proof of anything, rather than
as suggestive play in the manner of a poetic conceit), Irenaeus
is not concerned merely to suggest the parallelism of two
discrete, individual existences. He may well have thought there
was one particular man, Adam, who was directly created as
the first, lone human being, but the significance of both Adam
and Christ for him is that they may both represent us, any
of us, and manifest the catholicity of experience.

> For he came to save all through means of himself, all I
> say, who through him are born again to God — infants
> and children and boys and youths and old men. He
> therefore passed through every age, became an infant for
> infants, thus sanctifying infants, a child for children, thus
> sanctifying those who are of this age . . . a youth for

48

youths, becoming an example to youths, and thus sanctifying them for the Lord. So likewise he was an old man for old men, that he might be a perfect master for all, not merely as regards the setting forth of the truth, but also as regards age, sanctifying the aged also. Then at last he came on to death itself."

(*Adversus Haereses*, ll.4).

(The old age notion he arrives at, incidentally, by an interestingly Wittgensteinian piece of linguistic analysis. The Jews said to Jesus (John 8:55), "Thou art not yet fifty years old, and hast thou seen Abraham?". "Now," remarks Irenaeus, "such language is fittingly applied to one who has already passed the age of forty without having as yet reached his fiftieth year, yet is not far from that latter period. But to one who is only thirty years old, it would unquestionably be said 'Thou art not yet forty years old'. And then of course in a first century Palestinian context, or a second century Celtic one, it was probably uncontroversial to speak of 'past forty' as "declining into old age".)

At any rate, the crucial point, whatever the details of its establishment, is the suggestion that Christ, like Adam, is *representatively* human. Only in virtue of this can what becomes of him be properly taken as relevant to what may become of us, even paradigmatic for it. Were he merely himself as an individual, defined over against all others, one could appropriately say to his history 'So what?'. For Irenaeus, it is the fact that he sums up our humanness which makes him soteriologically significant, not any kind of extrinsic magic or judicial fiat of God.

This may seem a long way from the past and its undoing, but I take it to be worth lingering on for a moment, since 'representative humanity' is one of those phrases which theologians more often utter than elucidate. What can it possibly mean?

In the context of Atonement theory, the two commonest

Western models have been the quasi-legal substitutionary one (I go to be punished instead of you) and the quasi-infectious one (the contagion of immortality is passed on to the rest of humanity by one man's having caught it). We are, I trust, suitably embarrassed by accounts of corporate personality translated in terms of either of these models, since they insult either God's integrity or man's freedom.

Irenaeus uses various images of what goes on as Christ relives the life of man from beginning to end, at each critical point responding to God positively rather than negatively. It is like unknotting a knot which has been tied by bending the loops of the rope in the reverse order: it is grafting unfruitful life onto fruitful stock: it is moistening separated grains of wheat so that they cohere in a bakeable dough: and so on.

It is worth noting that none of the images implies the substantial abolition of what has gone before. The past is not damned. It is worked into something new, which is nevertheless characteristically *its* future. Read in isolation, the metaphors may sound like those of an impersonal process, but it is clear everywhere in context that Irenaeus does not want to speak of any mechanical or automatic transition from death to life:

> For it is clear that neither could we, being many, be made one in Christ Jesus without the water from heaven.

That water, a synonym for the presence of the Spirit in the baptismal act, is for Irenaeus a freedom-enhancing person, not an irresistible deluge. The insistence on the non-coerciveness of salvation nerves both his Christology, with its emphasis on the human freedom of Jesus, and his ecclesiology with its hostility to Gnostic concepts of election.

Iraneaus' understanding of the work of Christ as undoing the past therefore depends at least on the intelligibility of the notion of human solidarity which is not subpersonal, and I suspect that this is where the centre of any subsequent discussion must lie. Let me therefore try out three suggestions which may indicate my usage of the term. They are intended to distinguish an existentially convincing sense of representativeness from legal, formal accounts of the relations which I have already suggested have disastrous theological implications.

1. Some years ago, in the context of fairly intensive contact with Christian-Marxist friends, I lived for some months with a sense of insuperable shame about being an academic. All the criticisms of isolation from the grass-roots of painful existence at the top of an academic hierarchy feeding at the expense of the bottom seemed (and still seem at times) incontrovertible. About that time however, a man who must be nameless to spare his Messianic blushes came to give a lecture. I have forgotten both the title and almost every particular sentence. But I was at the time immensely struck by the painful and unsimplified integration made between minutiae of scholarship and massive issues of human justice and freedom.

    Hearing him, even when I neither understood nor endorsed the specific connections, I found myself thinking "Goodness, as long as that man exists as an academic we are all vindicated". This was not because any calculus could produce an overall plus by adding his merits and subtracting the ills of academe. Nor was it even that most academics could hope to imitate the man. And yet there was a sense, which almost made vicarious atonement lucid, that being part of the academic community was justified by his being a member of it, and by that being celebrated.

2. Or again, consider Lear or Hamlet as representatively human. They too are certainly not typical, or even repeatable. They are quite distinctly themselves,

differentiated, unmistakeable. And yet they clarify and seal something of what it is to be human by which we may orientate and identify ourselves. The fact that they are fictional characters is irrelevant, though it may be that art represents us better to ourselves at times than the clutter of sheer co-existence because it can eliminate distracting contingencies. But the same conviction might refer to an actual person — Thomas More or Martin Luther King — or anyone else who, by his belonging to the human race, modifies the identity of each of us. It is in fact an extension of this possibility which makes Dostoevsky insist that any of us represents all of us, and that only dullness of perception makes us deny that in any saint or sinner we confront our own possibility as human.

3. Buber, in characterising the I-Thou relation, suggests that any genuine Thou fills the heavens and is inclusive. "This does not mean that nothing exists except himself. But all else lives in his light." This sense of one person or one thing representing the being of the world is most characteristically experienced in love or death. It can, of course, be written off as psychopathology, but I decide rather to take such contexts seriously as crucial indicators of ontology. Commonly, bereaved people with no theories about how they should feel, or even with theories that they should feel differently, simply report that they either cannot believe, or resent the fact that others are still alive, or flowers still growing. The isolability of the given world from the person now not given is cosmological nonsense.

The ontology which might make such instances cohere is one which abolishes the notion of identity as self-contained, atomic individuality. Even on the level of establishing public correlates of identity it is clear that our particularity cannot be described in terms of physical or psychic privacy, but requires a whole network of relations — what we have eaten, the state of our blood, who our parents are, where we live, whom we love or hate, what we are afraid of, what we hope for. Most specifically our peculiarly *personal* identity, more unique than any grid of human species-characteristics can locate is, on this view, essentially relational. It is defined by who finds us irreplaceable, who in freedom finds our loss intolerable for their own being.

The specifically Christian ontology of persons, if I read Irenaeus and company aright, is the suggestion that the identity of anything or anyone is its irreplaceability in the distinctive relation to God represented by Christ's relation to him. That is not for us a *natural* relation: it is not established by our mere biological existence, for that would undercut our personal freedom. Nor is it established by any necessity of God's nature (as Process Theology, I suspect, suggests) for that would undercut God. Rather it is a relation of freedom at both ends (so long as freedom on God's part is not presented as a choosing between options), in which God willingly identifies himself in relation to the whole of space-time creation.

For Irenaeus this is not for any of us a natural possibility, belonging as we do in historical Adamic time. For whatever actual context we are in — say, twentieth century Edinburgh's Scottish Presbyterian tradition, which space and time have distinctively moulded — we are effectively isolated from, say, eighth century BC Chinese, or our great-great-grandchildren, or even from contemporary Scottish Methodists. This possibility of isolation, sealed by death, and inherent in created existence has been actualised and reinforced by our responsible Adamic preference for going it alone.

It was no more a possibility, according to Irenaeus, for a first century Jewish prophet or teacher, no matter how ethically conspicuous or theologically sound; and soteriology would have collapsed for him if Jesus could be isolated either from the creation he willingly represented, or from the God in relation to whom his identity was constituted. It is therefore only if Jesus does not *naturally* belong to the precarious world of Adamic time that he has the power to recapitulate its being in a new direction, to head it towards the eschatological identity it can be given by the freedom of God towards it. And yet it is only if he does belong to it *willingly* that he can realise that identity as a personal response of creation, not an alien destiny to which man is dragged by the scruff of his corporate neck.

With specific relation to time, just as Christ is not himself by himself, so the past which he takes on as his is not itself by itself, but as it is opened up to the present and future of the God who is,in a somewhat risky phrase, 'there already'. The risk is of provoking all sorts of problematic models of God straddling time with ten-league boots as though time were for him what it is for us, except that he could cover more of it, faster. This image of course has provoked many of the traditional puzzles of omnipotence, omniscience and human freedom, which need much slower elaboration. Here it should be clear that I assume, without defending as they need defending, the following suppositions:

a) that our time does not exist for God as part of his own context of being for, if it did, he could in principle be isolated from things, which would be his ungodding;

b) that it does exist for God as the context of our being, and that he therefore relates to it in freedom;

c) that his relation to it is a critical one, supportive of what sustains our distinctive identities in relation, and destructive of what separates, isolates and limits our relatedness, specifically of time's natural outcome in death;

d)   that the past is therefore for God never fixed, since
it is always liable to reopening in the new context
of the eschatological future which he offers the world
as its proper *Sitz im Leben*.

If this is so, and I would argue that unless it is so God and
man cannot be significantly differentiated, then the bringing
of the world to participate in personal relationship to God
involves undoing the fixity of the past. It is not, as I have
already insisted, *cancellation* of what has been, or been done.
Rather it is 'loosening it up', transforming it by denying that
its temporal isolation in the before-now is an absolute
parameter to its possibilities. For these are now its in-relation-
to-God-possibilities, and God is not restricted in his capacity
for relationship by the, to us, irretrievable pastness of the past.
"If I make my bed in Sheol, thou art there also" (Psalm
139:8).

If this is even dimly intelligible, a serious threat is posed to
the ontology which our culture, whose anthropology defines
us as isolable individuals, takes for granted. That is
embarrassing enough. To unpick our whole thought and
language in response to a frame of reference which we have
long since learned to regard as antique theological imperialism
is very demanding. The fact is that we live in a world
structured by its present language. The irony seems even
greater when one wants to plead that no special religious
experience is the origin and context of such theology, but
simply the analysis of our common world and what is wrong
with it. For the current language of our common world
frustrates diagnosis in the terms which Christian theology
suggests.

There are, however, points at which one might begin to
suggest analogues/analogies at least, contexts where people
already take seriously something like the undoing of the past.

There is, for instance, a fairly widespread psychoanalytic model of such transformation of reality, where the past is relived and emerges into the present and the future as a new thing. There is a socio-political model in the rewriting of history which goes on conspicuously or inconspicuously, not just in wicked Stalinist publications but among sober, reputable British historians. The past is not, of course, entirely of their making, but neither, as the Existentialists keep reminding us, is it a brute datum like a rock of given dimensions. There is the common encounter with art, where literature or the visual arts offer concrete resistance to time's robbery of identity:

> Yet do thy worst, old Time! Despite thy wrong
> My love shall in my verse ever live young.

And there is the pervasive recognition of post-Structuralist consciousness that anything can be dismantled and remade, given will and ingenuity.

In taking such examples it is important to insist that the alteration of the past is not to be translated simply into the re-perceiving of the past. It is only if these instances indicate directions of *ontological* shift that they deserve attention.

The same is true of yet another possible clarificatory situation, that of forgiveness. This can, of course, be construed simply as a matter of ethical magnanimity, or even of legal fiction. "Let us go on with things in spite of what has happened", or, more menacingly, "I will treat you as though you hadn't done X, though let it be perfectly clear to both of us that you jolly well have". Theologically, however, such accounts trivialise the matter, and quite fail to account for the correlative absolution which the forgiven one celebrates. *That* only makes sense if being forgiven is being offered a future quite unconditioned by the past. What has been done is not unreal, but it is such an abstraction from the future of relationship which the forgiver intends that he absolutely resists its claim to attention in the ongoing situation. As a performative act, not as a lapse of memory, he forgets the past. It may be that in this sense only God ultimately can forgive, since only he is unconstrained by the past, psychically or in any other way: and what we do to one another would be better termed 'willingness to forgive'.

At any rate, whether any of these suggestions increases the plausibility of the term 'undoing the past', the extraordinary temerity of Christian tradition is that it affirms not only that this may intelligibly happen, but that it has. The liturgical affirmation of the early church at least was that the undoing of the past had already taken place, whatever mopping-up operations remained to be completed. The fact that there was no manifestly objective transformation, for instance that dying hadn't stopped, was understood in terms of the Irenaen conviction that "the light does never enslave anyone by necessity". The delicacy of God offers the world, through the uncoercive presence of the church, time to receive his invitation in the direction of its secured freedom.

The church as it understands itself in relation to this soteriology is neither a sociologically explicable institution nor an accumulation of consolidated authoritative tradition, but a community living out of the future of God and already free from the past of death. Liturgy is nothing but the celebration of the presence of the future or, in the language of the trade, realisation of the eschaton. Thus a baptised child is said to have its death behind it, not ahead of it. Some eucharistic liturgies have no prayer of confession since the community is, as church, ahead of its own ambiguous, sinful existence: its state of needing forgiveness is an abstraction from its re-identified existence as the kingdom of God, concretised in the presence of the Christ who had already undone the grip of the past. Indeed that conviction is implicit in the apparently less provocative affirmation of the communion of saints. For if it is not only in tenuous memory that the dead are there with the living worshippers, then *ipso facto* the finality of the past — "they have died" — is being denied. And yet they have not not died.

It seems to me that all this sets an agenda rather than enables a conclusion. I have tried to suggest how one reading of Christ as representative of our humanness would, in conjunction with an account of his specific identity in relation to God — the intention of Incarnation language — allows us to de-isolate the past, to resist the finality of its givenness. The analogy between resisting the fixity of the past and the absoluteness of our separability from one another is crucial, and may even be a connection rather than an analogue.

It is obvious, however, that both suggestions put under massive strain any notion of 'Christian Empiricism', because by all, and not just the narrowest canons of empiricism, we look and feel quite separable, and the past seems unalterably conclusive, death being the lynch-pin of both nightmares. The main defensive response theologically in face of what is aggressively the visible case has often been a tendency to create an alternative world of 'spirituality', where ghostly communion goes on in publicly undetectable but quasi-parapsychological ways. Yes, you really are your empirical self, but there is an internal spiritual essence of you which is capable of communion with other such essences, whether embodied or not.

I suspect that while theology cannot suffer a knock-out by employing such a strategy, it is increasingly losing on points. For the thin spiritual self haunts less and less persuasively the nexus of concrete existence, and is liable either to be exorcised by Ryle or naturalised by Uri Geller and Co. There may *be* no good news. But if there is, it must be about the concreteness of people and the rest of creation being sustained or recovered.

It seems to me therefore, that to accept the empiricist mapping of the world and then to try inserting religious phenomena into it is a sadly self-defeating procedure. For it is not the data of empiricism, but its axioms which are defective, most centrally its conviction that a thing, and moreover a person, is properly itself by being identified in isolation from what is not itself, separable from it. The most radical agendum for philosophical theology at the moment — for me, the only one with the least hope in the present philosophical climate of rescuing faith from seeming an alternative to intelligence — is to identify the axioms embedded both in our lived and thought culture, and to see what kind of alternative axioms Christian tradition or traditions suggest. That will not, of course, settle the truth questions, but it may clarify what it is, and give an intellectual cutting edge to the pious conviction that Christianity makes a difference.

The claim that the past can be undone seems to me then a characteristic recognition point alerting us to how very different an account of existence Christian faith has classically given. ('Classical' is a partly historical description, partly an honorific accreditation of what I take as a primarily creative time in theology.) As Wittgenstein would have put it, "For a blunder in the empiricist game — that's too big". Nevertheless it is intentionally an account of this existence, not of some spooky supernatural plane, and can only be vindicated as it impinges on and relates to people's concrete, shared being. The problem of how isolable or intact we are as persons, or the past is for us, is not answerable by reference to any psychologically specialised 'religious experience', but is some kind of existential issue for common life.

I suggest, then, that talk of undoing the past is a direct corollary of talk about the freedom of God and our involvement in it. You may not want to talk in any of these ways but, if you want to use the latter categories, then I think the former cannot be avoided as long as one agrees that the structure of space and time are a major obstacle to our freedom while being constitutive of our selfhood. I am clear, however, that there is much further to go in wrestling for an intellectual framework which would articulate the point without sounding like gobbledygook, sure as I am that it needs wrestling for. That must be a corporate enterprise. I hope that the recognition of the need might provoke some kind of collaborative wrestling, within the churches and beyond them, as to how the reality of God and the reality of time connect.

VI

In defence of disorder⋆

Let me begin by quoting a poem from Norman MacCaig's collection, *The World's Room*:

Between two nowheres
I have a small chaos in my house —
a thing easy to come by. I've not
tamed it, housetrained it.
No: I do my best
to enrage it, to cure it of a persisting small
infection of reason. I say to it
come on, be chaotic! Make the door of my room
    open
on the door of my room. That painting above the
    fireplace
why shouldn't its birds fly off or land
on its own water, splashing the hearth tiles?
And me — why should I cross the room, why
shouldn't it cross me?
But all it can do
is push my spectacles under a cushion,
change dates in a letter, put an empty glass
in the chair I'm just sitting down in:
I reach for the book by my side
and it's been hijacked to the kitchen.
I say, Come on, you can do better than that!
until I can get so lost in this room search-parties
have to be sent out for me, until I see what's
    behind me
more clearly than what's in front of me — until you

⋆ First published in *Theology*, September 1977

crack the sad articulations
in my mind.
How can I make something new, something
crammed
with dangerous, beautiful possibilities —
something remarkable even if only for
its excess of normality?
We praise the good God for his creation
of the universe.
When are the hymns to be written
in praise of the unimaginable power of the word
that first made the chaos
that made creation possible?

In most theological circles, such a sentiment would, if taken seriously at all, be regarded as subversive for, it is commonly held, God is behind order. This almost standard apologetic assumption is testified to by generations of Gifford lecturers, who have moved from claims of either moral or natural order in the world to infer at least the probability of God. In countless mythologies he is the one who has subdued the great monster of chaos; in philosophical theology he is the postulated origin of the detectable design in things, and in moral-political terms he is the one who, *ceteris paribus*, supports the ordering of society.

As late (and as liberal) as John XXIII's *Pacem in Terris* one finds:

Human society can be neither well-ordered nor prosperous unless it has some people invested with legitimate authority to preserve its institutions and to devote themselves as far as is necessary to work and care for the good of all. These, however, derive their authority from God.

Admittedly he goes on to speak of the conditions of just authority, but that he can start where he does is a significant index of the tradition, a synthesis ironically documented in Brecht's *Life of Galileo*:

> When the Almighty ordered his great Creation,
> He told the sun that it, at his command,
> Must circle round the earth for illumination
> Just like a little maiden, lamp in hand.
> For it was his desire each thing inferior
> Should henceforth circle round its own superior.
> And things began to turn for all their worth,
> The lesser ones around the greater,
> And round the earlier the later,
> As it is in heaven, so on earth.
> And round the Pope revolve the cardinals,
> And round the cardinals revolve the bishops
> And round the bishops revolve the secretaries,
> And round the secretaries revolve the magistrates,
> And round the magistrates revolve the craftsmen
> And round the craftsmen revolve the servants
> And round the servants revolve the dogs, the
>   chickens and the beggars.
> That, good people, is the Great Order.

Few people now, outside the Monday Club, believe that natural and political order so hang together, but the conviction had deep cultural roots. The ancient art of soothsaying linked natural disorder to political disaster. (Caesar should not go to the Capitol, for the omens are strange.) The hierarchical structures of Feudalism and the divine right of kings presupposed similar connections (cf Ulysses' "O when degree is shaked" speech in Shakespeare's *Troilus and Cressida*) and more loosely the conviction persisted into the complacency of:

> The rich man in his castle,
> The poor man at his gate;
> God made them high or lowly
> And ordered their estate.

Unobtrusive common speech suggests remnants of the synthesis; 'law and order', 'the moral order', are still used without embarrassment by many: various sexual practices or types of violence are still often called 'unnatural'. All are relics of the perspective which allowed Hobbes to call true moral philosophy "the science of the laws of nature".

On the whole, however, the supposition is pretty well exhausted in modern European thinking. Since the breakdown of feudalism, or Grotius' plea to free international law from theology, or Kant's massive separation between cosmic order and self-legislating ego, increasing weight has been given to the idea that, in the moral and political sphere, law does not reflect order, but *generates* it. Laws, then, are conventions, implicitly or explicitly worked out within society on roughly Utilitarian grounds for the well-being of most of its members. No cosmic violation would be involved should we drive on the right rather than on the left; it is merely a matter of mutual practical convenience that we have such laws.

Where laws relate to moral issues (eg killing or theft or infringement of liberty) there is less agreement that the law is mere convention. Even so, within the context of moral philosophy, the 'conventionalist' understanding of morality has moved up from being a scandalous outsider (as when Hobbes was anathematised in churches) to being a front runner. While far from being obsolete, the notion of an intrinsic moral order is clearly under pressure.

Even in philosophy of science, some bold (or rash?) spirits suggest that, in the natural world too, order may be a function of our seeing or choosing to look in a certain way. Common sense puts up harder resistance to the allegation that the order in nature isn't 'really there', but one does not have to go very far in that philosophy of science to realise how easily we incorporate questionable 'axioms' in many acts of perception. One need not be an extreme sceptic, or even an extreme idealist, to take seriously the possibility that at least some of what we take to be the order 'in things themselves' is in fact a result of our schematising modes of apprehension.

For much of its history, Christian apologetics has felt bound to resist such suggestions in the spheres both of nature and of morality, since the establishment of order in the world has been assumed to be relevant to the defence of God's existence. There may have been frequent doubt whether order was in *fact* detectable (hence the intensity of the Hume-Paley debate, or the current nervousness in some theological quarters about the implications of sub-atomic randomness). It has, however, rarely been questioned that *were* there a clear, demonstrable order in things, that would be one up for God and one down for atheism. The heyday of this conviction was probably Deism, where God became almost nothing but the underwriter of various alleged orders; but it persists both in the formal mode of the Argument from Design, and more casually in the feeling that orderliness in the world strengthens the case for God's existence.

The MacCaig poem suggests another theological possibility (though MacCaig might call himself an atheist), one which has become completely submerged in our Western tradition. The alternative, in short, is that the order of the world should be treated theologically not as an aspect of Creation or Providence as such, but as an aspect of 'Fallenness'. This must be distinguished from the Gnostic view that matter itself is evil, or Creation identical with Fall (a view, incidentally, which Tillich's doctrine of 'existence' curiously resembles). Rather it is the suggestion that the specific *condition* of material existence, namely its subjection to causal necessity, is not a constitutive condition of matter as such, but of matter in a fallen world. ("The bondage of corruption" — Rom 8.21; "principalities and powers" — Eph 6.12; "the elements of the world" — Col 2.20, etc.) Patristic exegesis of such phrases suggests that one should see necessity, causality and the inevitability of cause and effect not as a ground for celebration, but as something evil, which has the world in its grip.

The heart of the theological critique of such aspects of

existence is the realism of the relation between order and death. Precisely the natural processes which constitute the world, constitute it a dying world. Age, decay, dissolution, the capacity for disintegration, are invariable concomitants of the order which structures our existence.

The realism of the perspective has strong endorsement from modern science, eg from A R Peacocke in *Science and the Christian Experiment*. He documents in detail the absolute interconnection between biological mechanisms of survival and destruction on different levels of existence. Given the processes that make life possible in this part of the universe, death is inevitable in that part, in that the survival of some organisms has to be at the expense of others. Everything hangs together. As scientist, Peacocke is prepared to argue that we could not have anything resembling this cosmos without the presence of death as we know it.

As theologian he goes further, suggesting that we are constrained to accept that things are so, not simply in recognising (in the weak sense) that what is the case is the case, but by *endorsing* or welcoming its being so. In theological terms, this means placing the givenness of the actual world, death and all, as part of the givenness of creation, a providential aspect of God's loving will. With thorough consistency, Peacocke argues that even human death, though psychologically distressing to man *in situ*, has to be theologically accepted as the necessary concomitant of the world's life.

In summary form, the argument runs:

Order and death are inevitably linked
Order has to be accepted as a condition of the
    universe being itself.
Therefore death has to be accepted as a condition of
    the universe being itself

The 'alternative theology' reverses the argument:

Order and death are inevitably linked
Death *cannot* be accepted as a condition of the universe being itself
Therefore order *cannot* be accepted as a condition of the universe being itself

Death, from this perspective, is no domesticable fact of life, but its antithesis, the condition of the universe losing its identity, not a constituent of that identity. The order of causal necessity, the processes to which the world is empirically subject, cannot then be construed as part of the providential will of God who is life and the antithesis of death. That order, culminating naturally in the eventual dissolution of things, is an aspect of the world's predicament, not of its created excellence. It is that from which things have to be rescued.

This is, of course, far more the instinct of the poet or the lover than of the scientist trained to accept the given as the unique standard of the real. But it is a characteristic passion of art to fight off transience; love's war with the bloody tyrant, time, is central to the metaphysics of, say, Shakespeare's sonnets. In such contexts, the rule of the empirical *status quo* is resisted as a kind of ontological fascism; the order of time and death needs defying as much as the dictatorship of despots.

From such a theological base-line, many things change. Miracle, for instance, becomes not an inexplicable and somewhat arbitrary interruption by God of processes whose constancy he has already sanctioned, but a wresting of the world from the limitations of its subjection to causality — in mythological terms the restoration to the world of the freedom it had before the Fall — or the anticipation of its eschatological future.

(I say 'in mythological terms' because the position does not seem to me to depend logically on the historical affirmation that there actually was a concrete empirical time when the world was free from the constraint of necessity. What it does insist on is that the bondage of necessity must be placed theologically not as an aspect of Creation, but as an aspect of the problem of evil. The indisputable fact that "this is how things are" is no more a ground for satisfaction with them in the natural than in the political realm.)

Probably the nearest exponents of such resistance in our contemporary culture are the existentialists, though there is a significant distinction between the form of their opposition and that of the Byzantine or Russian form. All share the insistence that man cannot properly understand himself as a naturally determined organism, whether the determinism is biological, psychological or sociological. He accepts that account only in *mauvaise foi*. For existentialism, he knows himself truly only in his decision made in radical freedom to transcend the order which lays claim to his identity. (Secular/humanist and Christian existentialists disagree of course as to whether the resources for self-transcendence lie wholly within the individual, but that has no particular relevance here.)

This western mode of existentialist thinking differs in two ways from the Eastern position:

i)   it assumes that the moral self (ie the self capable of an act of pure will apart from the conditions of its embodiedness) is itself

ii) it happily leaves the world of nature and the past to the reign of determinism

Eastern traditions (whether Hebrew, Greek or Russian), seeing this tendency as one towards spiritualising Gnosticism, are more realistic about the first point, and therefore have to be bolder and more incredible on the second. They affirm:

i)   that a person is not himself as spirit or will or as

anything other than body, so that contemporary Existentialism involves fantastic abstraction

ii) that, consequently, any postulation of salvation/ authenticity, etc. for persons must involve the recovery of freedom for the natural world as well (cf the imagery of mountains skipping, lions and lambs lying down together, death losing its grip, space and time as we know them no longer defining our existence — ie resurrection)

The alternative eschatology then suggests that, even in the realm of nature, the order of things will be undermined quite radically. There will be earth, but a new one.

Massive problems face anyone wishing to defend such a position. Some are characteristic of any theological assertion, others are peculiar to this theme.

In the first category come all the difficulties about cashing the mythological cheque. To say what it means — referentially that God ratifies disorder of a certain sort — is no easier than to explain the claim that he ratifies order. How does one distinguish 'order exists' from 'God ratifies order'? Future pie-in-the-sky, orderly or disorderly, seems equally remote. Past pie in a prelapsarian Paradise or a postlapsarian Palestine is equally inaccessible; and the present life of the Church hardly gives a reference point for eschatological confidence.

More important in this context are the theological difficulties internal to the position outlined above. How does one specify the difference between the freedom from order, which is here suggested as one element of salvation, and sheer chaos? Can the creativity of God's relation to the world be specified except by analogies from causal ordering? I find the best place to look for comparisons is in the realm of aesthetics.

It is interesting that classical Greece, with its conviction of the inexorability of law (making tragedy the necessary mode of the exercise of human freedom) also gave Europe the category of 'order' as central to its aesthetic appreciation. The axiomatic status of this category, however, may be challenged.

In a Paul Klee exhibition, the title *The Order of Things* stood over his paintings as a playful and ironic tribute to the artist's capacity to unpick the world and remake it. Constantly, in relation to time, artists understand themselves as resisting the givenness of process: Sterne's *Tristram Shandy* in the comic mode, Keats' *Grecian Urn* or Shakespeare's sonnets in the tragic. Similarly, possibilities of flashback in film, or stream of consciousness in the novel, defy the sequence of objective documentary time. The visual arts similarly undermine space: Soutine's houses defy the laws of gravity, not to mention the more extreme antinomianisms of cubism or abstract painting. So too with dance: a French ballet critic, Emile Vuillemoz, writing in *La Revue Musicale* of December 1921, described the acrobatic manual of the 18th century *haute ecole* Russian ballet:

> Of course that superior technique required a systematic emancipation from all the constraints of our humble earthly condition so as to move towards an ideal of agility, rapidity, nimbleness and superhuman balance.

There are, however, limits. The art is not without form in any of these cases. The substance (paint, marble, human muscle, etc.) imposes constraints. But it seems to me at least as plausible to 'read' the artist, like MacCaig, as aspiring towards the abolition of these limits rather than cherishing them as conditions against which he sharpens his creative powers. (There is an interesting political parallel here in the question emerging from Marxist dialectic: must causality be welcomed or hated as the condition defining man's political responsibility?) What is significant about the artist (as Buber well documents) is that their distinctive mode of relating to the environment or the material produces something unrepeatable — a quite different notion of 'cause' from the normal scientific one, susceptible as it is to experimental repetition or universalisability. (Not even quantum theory has undermined scientific confidence in the experimental repeatability of processes, which are normally called 'causal'.)

It may be merely a semantic matter whether one calls this unique creativity of the artist 'order' or 'disorder'. Certainly it is not chaos, and equally certainly it is not specifiable according to law. It makes a unique world, and in that respect seems not a bad image for what creativity means in the context of God-talk. We would probably now say it was strictly a 'pathetic fallacy' to think of the stone responding to the sculptor; but that metaphor seems to be the one which explores the fantasy of earlier Christians on the 'original' condition of creation. The cosmos responded to invitation with a variety of willing existence in which no element of coercion was present; it offered no resistance to the imagination of God.

We know/believe that there was no historical time under these conditions. But the role of myth is to legitimise the most radical dissatisfaction with the limits imposed on us by letting us yearn for the condition which would make us most ourselves. It is correlative with our choice to see ourselves properly identified not by our limiting boundaries, but by their removal — or even by the longing for their removal. It endorses the discrimination which the doctrine of the Fall requires in Christian tradition, that our condition of existence is not co-terminous with the Kingdom of God.

Most Christian theology has paid lip-service to this doctrine, but in essentially unrealistic ways. Firstly, they have limited the identification of fallenness to the moral, assuming the questionable doctrine of the radical autonomy of the will over all other aspects of personality. And then, with Existentialism, they have identified salvation with some kind of obliteration of the past, as if the New Man were quite discontinuous with the old — a position which becomes effectively a gnostic, not a Christian, account of the Fall.

Curiously, the analysis of what I here call disorder, this antinomian creation in the context of unique relations, involves

71

no departure from many central Christian affirmations which have survived in our modern European tradition. It simply challenges the mode of interpreting these affirmations. For instance, we commonly affirm the reality of God's forgiveness. But if we also believe that such forgiveness constitutes someone's identity rather than denying it (cf the debate about retribution in moral philosophy where it is sometimes argued that not to punish is a violation of man's identity and dignity) then we are *ipso facto* involved in challenging the determinism of causality. This of course in no way proves that Christianity is not total fantasy; it merely suggests that the fantasy is more consistently worked out if we envisage the order of natural law as an aspect of Fall rather than of Creation.

The 'unlawbound' creativity, which is the alternative to disorder that I have so far offered, is one analogy from aesthetics. Another (but almost a cliche for theologians) is the creativity which one person exerts on another. Again, Buber documents how resistant real human relationship is to analysis in causal terms. We are notoriously different people to different people, and only a total reductionism would try to describe that variety as the statistical play of genes on genes. In various contexts — eg counselling or the theological anthropology of Pannenberg — the elusiveness of a real person is being insisted on as phenomenologically crucial. And — taking either the artist-freed work of art, or the person-freed person seriously as paradigms of reality — we are involved, it seems to me, in some kind of negative stance toward whatever qualifies such freedom.

As the allegation of God behind order supported conservative political stances, so this theological myth may provide a more integrating context for dissatisfaction with various aspects of the *status quo* — ie for intuitions of God in the political mode, like Barth's certain conviction that his teachers' endorsement of the Kaiser's war policy had to be resisted. It may indeed be that the reiterated ecclesiastical backing of political establishment has had more to do with politics *tout court* than with theology. If, however, there are theological grounds for dissatisfaction with the given structures of human existence, then it is less easy for faith to sleep so promiscuously with acceptance of the *status quo*.

When one works from the basic premise that the natural order of the world is an aspect of Providence, then the concomitant distresses have to be laid at God's door. If such order, on the other hand, is properly seen as an ontological limit to the world's possibilities, then God becomes an 'ally' (to speak anthropomorphically) in the battle to free things from their restrictedness and perishability, and not a limit to that struggle.

All this may, at worst, be the projection of a maverick temperament onto the Almighty. I take it rather as elaboration of the one fact that love cannot accept what it loves dying; it is impossible to welcome with one hand the law-death syndrome, the minimal structure of order, and on the other really to love (or, if the word is too cluttered with sentimentality, to be significantly creative).

This negative placing of order which I recommend for theological attention would affect the whole range of attitudes and political stances we take to the artist, the criminal, the madman, the State, the Church, the university, the limits of our nature, and perhaps (though this will be my last ditch) the law of non-contradiction. At any rate, it strikes me currently as one of the few theological suggestions I have encountered which combines realism about how-the-world-is with the refusal to identify that with how-God-wants-it-to-be. In this respect it gives scope to a restlessness which, if consolidated, may be creative.

VII

The strangeness of the Church

The Church is, of course, odd. As the late Dr Archie Craig, a distinguished former Moderator of the General Assembly of the Church of Scotland, was wont to quote from a secular colleague: "Sometimes, you know, the church is a re-re-revolting institution".

That needs no documenting. The Orthodox doctrine of the sinlessness of the Church seems therefore to involve a redefinition of terms, or a total dissociation between 'true Church' and 'actual Church'. For the institution which has stumbled through the history of the last two-thousand years, ragged and stained with complicity in much evil, is manifestly not sinless. Indeed, its claim to be the concrete bearer of God's mission to the world seems to many so implausible as to make the very notion of a God with a mission *more* questionable than it might have been without the Church. For many radicals, if God gets through to the world, it is *in spite* of the church, not because of it. Belonging to the church is more problematic than belonging to the world.

Yet the strangeness of the church, as distinct from its oddity, is that it is called to be the concretion of God's 'alternative society', manifesting and earthing the future of the cosmos, the kingdom of God.

The question of how one lives without schizophrenia, between the sense of church as the bearer of eschatology to time and the awful pain of its recurrent failure, is no slick conundrum with a known answer.

My concern in this essay is to suggest, more specifically, some of the 'marks of the church', by which, surely, the *de facto* institution stands to be judged and the church's fidelity recognised.

There are, of course, delicate questions on the boundary

between sociology and theology as to what *counts* as the church, for 'church' is one of those categories which might illustrate what is meant by an 'essentially contested concept'; that is to say, its history across time means that it can be appraised from a variety of standpoints, that there are conflicts as to what are the necessary and sufficient conditions for defining it, and that there are no 'independent' vantage points outside particular hermeneutical circles for appraising it. (*The Nature of Belief*, Chapter 9, Elizabeth Maclaren, Sheldon Press, 1976.)

The most robust if drastic solution to the problem of the church's identity is, of course, to stipulate one single article of faith and/or practice as the *articulus stantis et cadentis*, the necessary and sufficient condition for being Christian, and to dismiss the rest. The strategy has been commonly employed, sometimes with deliberately restrictive precision, sometimes with generous eirenic intention. "Only those who admit the *homoousios* are of the true church", "Anyone baptised may share in communion", "Only those fighting actively on behalf of the poor belong to the community of the faithful", and so on. The trouble, obviously, is that most of these criteria either eliminate an uncounted percent of the people who have historically wanted to call *themselves* Christian, or they risk blurring so many different positions as to say nothing significant at all.

The question is not just a philosophical one about the identity of things for the purposes of intellectual gratification. It is one for which, as we well know, countless Christians have thought it worth dying . . . and even killing: one which has certainly caused immense pain and anxiety as people wonder with whom they stand, and against whom. Luther would not share the Lord's Table with Zwingli after the Marburg Colloquy, because it seemed to him that somehow, in the definition of the real presence in the Lord's Supper, salvation was at stake. And we, with our relativist awarenesses, who find it grotesque that a doctrine should be taken so seriously that we would not eat with someone who disagreed with us, cannot afford to be disparaging. It is not necessarily the act of bigoted fanatics lining up behind facile theological banners, but of people who feel the relation between truth of speech and truth of being is crucial and not to be trivialised. Similar intensity and passion divides people today over, say, the ordination of women or the need for confessional orthodoxy. And it lies behind the painful inability, so unintelligible to most liberal ecumenical Protestants, of Roman Catholic and Orthodox Christians to share the eucharist with those they cannot truthfully identify as sharing a common faith and order.

It is culturally easy for those who sit more loosely to official creeds, to suggest the limited value of judging anyone's Christian identity in terms of whether or not he is willing to say a given set of words, and to deplore the sectarianism which is entirely a matter of slogan encountering slogan and people missing people.

To judge Christian identity in terms of how people *behave* may be equally inept, though it is possibly more tempting to many. This is true not only because the traditionally implied ways of behaviour are extraordinarily difficult to pin down, but also because the distance between the inwardness of an action's motivation and intention and the externals of its performance may be immeasurably large. If we believe at all that we live *simul iustus et peccator*, we cannot judge ourselves or others by achieved excellence.

This sounds suspiciously like saying "There is no way of judging what is church", a position which may be a salutary corrective to complacent exclusivism, but it does not help much with those who are seriously wrestling with issues of discipline, ecumenical hospitality or mutual recognition of ministry and sacrament. Nevertheless, there is a sense in which agnosticism about what counts as church may be affirmed, not as a piece of woolly-minded *laissez-faire* liberalism, but as an implication of the eschatological surprisingness we should be learning to live with as a sign of God's strangeness and challenge to our structures.

If the primary identity of the Church is an eschatological one, perhaps the most important recognition about it is that we do *not* presently know all that it will mean to have our Christian identity established. "We do not know what we shall be." This is an implication of the very fact that the Church is the community of those willing to have their humanness and the life of creation opened up towards the freedom of God and, therefore, to renounce the boundaries of their intact-so-far established identity. This seems to me to mean that we are bound to dissociate ourselves from attempts to define the Church primarily in terms of fixed, past tradition. Naturally, of course, we relate to our past. We owe it much. We may even believe that, at its best, it has been faithful to the vision of God's future which is our core identity; has been, in some sense the bearer of God's redemption, and belongs to the kingdom. But we do not belong to the vision, or the kingdom, in virtue of a stateable past which is closed, for when the past has been worth its salt (and not encouraging a fossilising concentration on history) it has itself been pointing to the future, and looking for its own enlargement in creativity.

It is not, however, any old future.

The uncertainty as to who we shall be is, for the Christian church, specifically related to the claim that who we are is "hid with God in Christ". Christian belonging in life and sacrament is the re-identification of our natural selves and our natural structures of belonging in relation to the eschatological man, the risen Christ ahead of us. That he too has a past is, as Irenaeus would have said, enough to sanctify the past, but as a past-open-to-transformation (the role that Resurrection/Ascension and Pneumatology variously play in New Testament Christologies). His primary identification, what makes him worshippable and not just venerable, is that he is the one who concretely brings the open future of God's strangeness to bear on the strangeness of being human.

77

Thus, in being related to him, we both know ourselves as having direction, bearing towards the maximal love-in-freedom which is the liveliness of God; and we do not know ourselves, because every encountered situation is liable to make us different as we open ourselves to it in the spirit of the one who will not say to anything in creation, "I am myself without reference to you".

This combination does not simply take us into a paradoxical fog in which inertia is the only possible response. For the identification, even if it cannot be fully specified, exerts pressure and leverage against us, absolutising our present belongings.

Many voices these days, from the world of inter-faith dialogue, from feminism, from the ecological and conservation lobbies rightly point out how disastrously 'the scandal of particularity' has sometimes affected Christian handling of others, whether it be pagans, Hindus, Muslims, women or other creatures and the natural environment.

This however happens, characteristically when the Christology involved is one of *exclusion* — Christ *versus* pagan, Muslim, etc. A quite different situation arises with a Christology which specifies that in this particular man there is the unique point in history, the anchoring so to speak of God's relating to everyone and everything. That, of course, may be no less offensive. Why on earth should God relate to Hindus via Christ rather than via their own heroes of faith and culture? An inclusive Christology may anger people with a sense of patronising dismissal of their traditions and indigenous apprehensions of God, just as an exclusive one may suggest a capriciously selective God. But we have to struggle, intellectually and of course practically, for an inclusiveness which is *not* dismissive.

It seems to me then that the 'scandal of catholicity', the fact that God wills and effects relationship to the whole earth in the earthed humanness of Christ, is a more important point for the church to start exploring its identity and mission. So far, the dominant way of understanding that purpose in Western traditions has often been in terms of an entitlement to active proselytising evangelism, since the assumption is made that free response to God in Christ involves conscious reaction to the Christian *message*. In a world newly recognising its vulnerability, and aware of how ideological conflict may hasten disaster, the Christian churches must, however, rethink their position. Is the style of uninvited intrusion into other cultures and their associated faiths really mission in the image of the Christian God? Are there not ways of confronting the world with the challenge of the gospel, other than saying "Acknowledge the name of Christ or be damned", ways which present deeper than verbal confrontation?

For to be so identified with the catholic Christ is not to stand in a mushy, "for he's a jolly good fellow" relationship to everyone and everything. As the strangeness of God resists our individualism, our possessiveness and our tendency to exclude and judge, so the strangeness of the Church has a critical relation to the world, in that it cannot embrace those who insist on defending their limited identity over against some other without offering a critique of that limitation. If I invite to my party both the leader of the Gay Liberation movement and Tony Higton (the Anglican priest who has bitterly condemned homosexuality), and if Tony Higton will not be seen dead in the company of a Gay Libber (or *vice versa*), then I cannot have both of them there: or at least if I can, it will no longer be a party, but more like a prison sentence for some. The recognition of the uncoerciveness of God's salvation must be the main caveat against any axiomatic universalism. Certainly it is a theological error to suppose there is anyone with whom God wills no relation in love. But the character of our response to his love of the others may make his relation to us critical. For he will not withdraw his invitation to our enemies to please our secure sense of boundaried identity: unless we are willing to have that broken open, we cannot want his presence or encounter it as joy, or have love-knowledge of Christ, whatever orthodoxies we utter.

The point is finely illustrated, in a quite secular idiom, in Patrick White's *Riders in the Chariot* (Eyre and Spottiswoode, 1961), where the four central characters in that novel are all in their own way open to the strangeness of new encounter. Each of them responds to people whom others have discarded or written off. But precisely because of that, each provokes immense hostility among the conventionally decent or pious. The central character is a Jew who has settled in Australia after escaping from a concentration camp. He now works in a factory making bicycle lamps, and one morning is greeted by the foreman:

'Howya doing, Mick?'
'Good,' replied the Jew, in the language he had learnt to use.
The foreman, who had already begun to regret things, drove himself still further. He was not unkind.
'Never got yourself a mate?' Ernie Theobalds remarked.
The Jew laughed. 'Anybody is my mate,' he said. He felt strangely, agreeably relaxed, as though it could have been true.
But it made the foreman suspicious and resentful.
'Yeah, that's all right,' he strained and sweated. 'I don't say we ain't got a pretty dinkum set up. But a man stands a better chance of a fair go if he's got a mate. That's all I'm saying. See?'
And further conversation is abruptly ended.

If the Church began to take seriously its identification in these terms, it would stand in our culture — and in any — as the most remarkable counter-culture phenomenon, defying sociological or psychological explanation. Simply consider the way we structure our social belonging. How many categories of normality/abnormality, insider and outsider we work with every day! Take, for instance, our classification and isolation of the mentally ill, over against whom we are labelled healthy. Yet how often are they representing the pain of lovelessness to which we 'healthy normal people' have less sensitivity? Or take our criminal justice procedures with their division between good citizens and bad. If we accept such definition of people, we are in effect saying that their past is more important to their identity than the future, that they *are* what they have done wrong. Indeed we operate with scores of categories of ethical or aesthetic self-esteem, our class systems, our party identifications, our alignments for or against this or that cause. Anyone who refuses to operate in those terms is a social oddity, even a danger. Yet if the Church took seriously even that one mode of identifying itself as a community which defies such distinctions, it would, I suspect, be dynamite again.

I do not think, however, that we can turn eschatology into ethics; that is to say, it is also an implication of being the Church that *in via* we currently live *behind* our possibilities, needing to recognise our limits and to confess that we have the most unsteady grasp of our eschatological strangeness. We have it in the penetration of word and sacrament, for instance, into the closedness of our existence, but we are still frustrated in finding all kinds of premature thresholds of will and capacity for living out of the openness of God. We huddle and align and moralise, as by insuperable instinct.

We are not yet able to be and do as we hope to be and do, though we glimpse it, taste it and see it growing sometimes. Yet we insist that our real identity is in the direction of our hope: which must mean that we can only live repentant, tangled up in compromises, but resisting self-judgment in terms of what we have managed, because we belong more intimately to our future than to our past.

This kind of criterion of eschatological identity serves as a critique of empirical Christian traditions, of the historical churches. For by such standards we can see the narrownesses and meannesses of Christendom as well as its occasional flashes of eschatological integrity. But the important thing is that it goes on drawing attention to the alternative possibilities of free and loving existence even when, or especially when, it does not manage to reflect them. That seems to me the nerve-centre of all prayer and liturgy. That may sometimes involve us in the paradoxical judgement that for whole tracts of its history the Church has failed to be, and fails to be, the Church.

But unless our ecclesiastical strangeness is our transparency to the generous strangeness of God, we lose all but trivial sociological interest for a world as fragmented and fragile as ours.

VIII

Belonging and not belonging

When preparing for a Student Christian Movement congress, in Keele in 1986, I looked at Bonhoeffer's *Ethics*, and found that a paragraph leapt at me from the page and shocked me to the core. It ran:

> Radicalism always springs from a conscious or unconscious hatred of what is established. Christian radicalism, no matter whether it consists in withdrawing from the world or in improving the world, arises from hatred of creation. The radical cannot forgive God his creation. He has fallen out with the created world ... When evil becomes powerful in the world, it infects the Christian too with the poison of radicalism. It is Christ's gift to the Christian that he should be reconciled with the world as it is, but now this reconciliation is accounted a betrayal and denial. It is replaced by bitterness, suspicion and contempt for men and the world. In the place of the love that believes all, bears all and hopes all, in the place of the love which loves the world in its very wickedness with the love of God, there is now the pharisaical denial of love to evil, and the restriction of love to the closed circle of the devout. Instead of the open church of Jesus Christ, which serves the world till the end, there is now some allegedly primitive Christian ideal of a Church which in its turn confuses the reality of the living Jesus Christ with the realisation of a Christian idea. Thus a world which has become evil succeeds in making the Christians become evil too. It is the same germ that disintegrates the world, and that makes the Christian become radical. In both cases it is hatred towards the world, no matter whether the haters are the godly or

83

the ungodly. On both sides, it is refusal of faith in the creation.

The shock was, of course, that this was Bonhoeffer writing; he was the man who, five years later, died for his active involvement in resisting Hitler, a hero of Christian radicals. It was not some theological acolyte of the New Right, sniffing out Marxism in the corridors of Canterbury: not some pietist academic saying Christianity and politics will not mix. Bonhoeffer endured the injuries of the Nazi regime with neither passivity nor compromise: he was involved in the conspiracy to assassinate Hitler. Yet it is from this man that we read

> "It is Christ's gift to the world that we should be reconciled to the world as it is"

> "It is the same germ that disintegrates the world, and that makes the Christian become radical"

I want to present those statements as a kind of provoking and questioning text over our exploration of this question of belonging and not belonging, of being square pegs in round holes, of Christian integrity and compromise.

Clearly, on the levels of psychology and sociology, there are 'belongers' and 'non-belongers'. Temperamentally — or by upbringing, political education or both — there are people who seem to go with the grain of things, as it were. They both feel and are easy with themselves and other people. They tolerate, with elation and good humour, almost every diversity of human conviction they meet; and even what they find distasteful they tend to tolerate or minimise. They are urbane, robust, unagonised and, in a way, immensely wholesome.

There are others who prickle and fret, who both seem to be and feel at odds with their existence, or aspects of it. They manifest a permanent restlessness, whose personal or cultural self-awareness is of marginality, and alienness to the received modes. The idea of being settled or at home in an average family, a typical suburb, a political culture, an existing church is inconceivable. They are born 'outsiders', the disturbers of any *status quo*. They are the aliens, and sometimes the alienated. In church terms, they are the prophets.

Even on the psychological or sociological level, the assessment of such stances is, of course, a matter of perspective. I remember once, as a theology student in a course on Theology and Psychiatry, being asked to do an Eysenck personality inventory for introversion/extroversion, and for neurosis. As the tutor handed out the questionnaires he said "Of course, you must remember that what Eysenck classifies as neurotic is what other people would mean by alive!".

Analogous differences of political temperament and strategy occur. There are those in any large-scale political community who feel that most is to be gained pragmatically by avoiding confrontation in principle. They learn to 'play the system', recognising the rules and the limits they impose, but maximising the opportunities for creativity within those limits. Others are convinced that the price is too high if you accept the presuppositions of the system. They are attracted or committed to the risks of confrontation politics, where you may blow up the whole network of accepted assumptions, so long as you do not compromise on the issue at stake. Perhaps the classic polarisation is between Christ and the Grand Inquisitor in *The Brothers Karamazov*, but it recurs in most personal mini-maps drawn from immediate experience of global, national, university or domestic politics!

As is the case with most other aspects of human existence, these differences between typical belongers and non-belongers have no doubt multiple explanations from many directions, many of them non-rational — one's infantile potty-training, one's physiology (glands and hormone levels), one's formative religious education, peer-group pressures, masked sexual frustrations, etc. It has even been suggested that such differences are a function of climate, like the difference between a Bergman film and a Rossini opera! My concern is whether we can find a way to read these differences theologically. Is it simply a matter of taste or style, occurring within our large freedom to explore the world with all our diversity of responses: like whether one prefers spinach or broccoli with roast chicken, or whether one enjoys Bach more than Bartok? Or is it a matter of fidelity or infidelity to the Kingdom of God, and to our invitation into positive relationship to that Kingdom?

The core of the Christian gospel is a promise and an invitation to belong in, to be at home in, the abolition of all exclusiveness, in sharing the outgoing life of a non-excluding God with the whole of creation. That, I think, challenges us to discover a new identity: it links us so generously and openly with one another, and with the cosmos, that we do not quite literally know who we are, or who we shall be. We drown in the depths of our future. One may use various provocative images but no maps. We will be related as intimately to those currently estranged from us by history, geography or ideology as the people we currently live with lovingly. There will be no coercion or constraint about our existence or how it impinges on others. There will be no-one of whom or to whom we can say: "I have nothing to do with you". There will be dilemmas, no options excluding options, no division of will posed by the desire to be with X and not with Y who is somewhere else. What the theological trade calls eschatology is the story of the future, the vision of how we end up! And we now live out the presence and the absence of that future.

Now that is a controversial theological allegation. I learn it from a certain reading of the New Testament and of the freedom of the risen Christ and the Communion of Saints. It strikes many of my friends, both Christian and non-Christian, as a sort of grotesque nightmare. And it strikes me as fairly terrifying. For I *do* belong, more or less happily, in all sorts of relatively closed, specific groups. My nuclear family, my cultural background of Western University education, my *Guardian*-reading 'intelligent left' political sympathies, my level of mildly ecological involvement about food and waste, my unsacrificial sympathy with the peace movement. I am, as it happens, timid about, or even on the defensive about communes, barbarians, Militant Tendency, vegetarianism, as well as being hostile to the stockbroker belt, *The Daily Telegraph*, NATO and foxhunting! What then does it *mean* to say that I believe I am called into the Kingdom of God? Can I integrate in any way my limited, concrete existential relationships as a politically pinkish, moderate, white Anglo-Saxon Protestant with what I say about this explosion of identity involved in being "hidden with God in Christ"? Do I go schizophrenic? Do I renounce my present belongings? Do I relax into them as a justified sinner? Or do I hop uneasily from my eschatological toe to my uneschatological toe?

The question bites too on the life style of the church. In the circles in which radicals normally move, the dominant orthodoxy is clearly that it is the church's primary role to be prophetic, to be aligned, to denounce the failures of world and church in relation to peace and justice and to signal, by its exemplary and committed life, what it would mean to accept the rule of God; to abandon its wealth and status, for instance; to steward the world with equity.

Churches which say 'All welcome' are suspect, charged with presenting a form of 'cheap grace' which is either merely verbal or sentimentally superficial. They massage their ingrained and comfortable *laissez-faire* liberalism, oiling it with universality texts, missing all the 'unlesses' of the Gospel and all sense of the outrage of God at our structures of exploitation and corporate selfishness.

I am sure that the suspicion is proper since the slack complacency of the churches in the prosperous world is one of our greatest treacheries. Nevertheless, I think we need a much more delicate and corporate assault on the question of what is distinctive about *Christian* prophecy: how does it (does it?) square the circle of eating both with the Pharisees and the Publicans? (Most of us have temperamental and structural affinities with one lot or the other. But to belong, with integrity, with both — that is really worrying!) How do we enact and manifest the acceptance and love of God, not just to the oppressed, the marginalised, the alien, whom we easily identify as *deserving* it, but to the ones we know *don't*, to the exploiters and the spoilers of life?

At the same time, I am more and more haunted by another evangelical suggestion, though it causes such disruption to my ethical self-confidence that I can hardly say I welcome it. That is the sense that, as we grow towards the holiness of God, we *stop* judging others. Can one be a non-judgemental prophet?

It is interesting, especially speaking from within Scottish culture with all its history of Puritanism and stern morals, that there is a strong secular reaction against the judgementalism of our Calvinist past which has wide acclaim. Is that, I wonder, simply that the *areas* judged are felt to have been inept and life-denying? Or is it a deeper critique, with which Christians ought to have deep imaginative resonance, that all our judging of one another, in whatever context, signals our dehumanised distance from God?

Here, for instance, is a characteristic poem from the Scottish poet, Iain Crichton Smith, drawing with his attentive sense of the crippling of it, the austerity of West Highland Presbyterianism:

Old Woman

Your thorned back
heavily under the creel
you steadily stamped the rising daffodil.

Your set mouth
Forgives no-one, not even God's justice
perpetually drowning law with grace.

Your cold eyes
watched your drunken husband come
unsteadily from Sodom home.

Your grained hands
dandled full and sinful cradles.
You built for your children stone walls.

Your yellow hair
burned slowly in a scarf of grey
wildly falling like the mountain spray.

Finally, you're alone
among the unforgiving brass
the slow silences, the sinful glass.

Who never learned,
not even ageing, to forgive
our poor journey and our common grave,

while the free daffodils
wave in the valleys and on the hills
the deer look down with their instinctive skills

and the huge seas
in which your brothers drowned
sing slow over the headland and the peevish crow.

It is not difficult for those brought up in the permissive
liberalism of the sixties and seventies to deplore such severe
renunciation of common humanness — especially in areas
normally defined as a matter of 'personal freedom' or

individual lifestyle. Yet very commonly, the same people who are able and willing to be relaxed about the fallibilities and limitations of others in private life, and even able to identify with them, at least in sympathy and imagination, cannot bear to recognise in themselves the possibilities of isolation and brutality thrown up in South Africa or Northern Ireland or in the Lebanon.

What is ironic about the goody/baddy polarisation of distancing oneself politically from someone is that it is easily masked as engagement, and not at all recognisable as the fey, otherworldly dissociation of asceticism or pietism. Yet dissociation happens even at the good barricades!

When I was cutting my theological teeth in the sixties, it was reaction to spiritualised dissociation from the corrupt world which was the dominant theological mood. To be properly embedded in the underclass, to belong, to take sides, to be a member of the secular city was the only legitimate response for the incarnationally-minded Christian. Only here, in the concrete struggle to make life more just, more free, more comradely, could Christians be the Church. Liberation theologies of various sorts sustain that agenda today, with an urgency which is clearly truthful, and often a passion which is costly.

It was of course a wonderful, exhilarating, exuberant time in which to be a student, with massive hope that, in a measurable time, the world was transformable. It was as exciting as the crusades — but, maybe, also as self-righteous. Its theological failure was, I suspect, to fail to register any distance whatsoever between certain forms of political involvement and the coming of the Kingdom of God. Eschatology was to be realised by a clear political agenda.

Now, if the first mis-belonging is dissociation, this total identification is, I suspect, simply a form of paganism. The word may seem surprising, conjuring up as it does visions of exotic orgies on the South Downs or the boiling of missionaries in cooking pots. But I think the root of paganism is the identification of God as contained in the natural processes of the world, be they biological, political, historical or whatever. The Kingdom of God is a judgement on paganism, not because of the danger of the lunatic fringes of religious sensationalism, but because *settling for* the world's rhythms of individual, psychic, social and political flux will sandbag us against the explosion of the Kingdom.

I think this struck me most forcibly a few years ago when I saw an Australian film called *Manganini*. It was set in the Australian bush in the early 19th century, when an entire Aborigine tribe, excepting one woman, had been wiped out by white soldiers. This woman set off to find some others of her people, and, while living alone still, came upon a white family picnicking in the bush. The little girl, about eight years old, saw the woman and, attracted by her firestick, followed her. Eventually, after one abortive attempt at escape, the child stayed with the woman, uncoerced. The woman accepted the child as, in some way, a replacement for her people, and cherished her, teaching all the lore of the bush, and some of the language. Gradually the trappings of white civilisation wore out, the pink petticoats, the white leggings, the dainty shoes, etc., and the child was initiated into a new identity, a new mode of living with Manganini. At the end of the film, the woman knew that she was dying and returned the child to her parental home, where she had to begin to straddle the two worlds; but, as Manganini's corpse burned, it was clear that a child's belonging to the Aboriginal world was inalienable, and her father's world would have to come to terms with that.

Here were none of the stock associations of paganism — the vaunting *hubris* of physical prowess, the superstitious placating of alien powers. The woman's bearing in the world was dignified and tender, modest and steady, reverent but not deferential, with a quiet trust in her instinctual life and her senses. But it was this complete acquiescence in the natural ebb and flow of life and death, her belonging there without resistance which seemed to me to present the seductive menace of the position.

For the presence of the Kingdom of God is, I believe, disruptive of the natural ebbs and flows which identify us; disruptive of death ultimately, and of all the mini-belongings in family, class, race, sex, nation, denomination, ideology which plough into death. And it is disruptive also, not just of the worst viciousnesses of our political co-existence, but of the best of it; for the realm of politics has to be the realm of constraints and sanctions and containment of what is disruptive to the political community, even when that community is about the greatest good of the greatest number. And such containment cannot be projected onto the freedom of the Kingdom.

Our distance from the Kingdom of God is not just a matter of our individual or corporate failure to will freedom or community, tragically clear as that failure is in a world containing Soweto, Sarajevo and the Shanklin Road. But even with the best will in the world, we find ourselves characteristically having to choose the lesser of two evils, nothing else being available: or having to choose one desirable manifestation of love and freedom but, in doing so, having to withdraw our energies from another desirable one.

This is particularly clear when we consider the relationships by which we *actually* identify ourselves both on the personal and the communal level. It is frightening to try doing an identity grid of oneself linking the networks of one's own belonging and asking whether any of them unambiguously sustain freedom or love. If the hole is Kingdom-shaped, all the pegs are square!

Indeed, I increasingly suspect that we are incapable of having natural or political structures of belonging which are not also structures of exclusion. This is not culpable. It is part of the fabric of being human — the part to which Christian tradition gives the name of 'fallenness', and which Paul calls earthenware pots! But it calls for transformation.

It is part of our ordinary experience, this ambivalence of belonging and excluding. Becoming a wife and mother has made possible for me some otherwise missed experience of free relationship, but immediately makes me less available for other kinds of relating to the ranges of possibility. Being a white British citizen, whatever my impeccable political convictions, puts me into a human sub-group, a belonging which is structurally responsible for the steady death by starvation of the Third World. Not all the buying of Oxfam Christmas cards will alter that. As well as moral, chosen factors, quite non-ethical factors frustrate the identification of our world with the Kingdom of God. After a certain amount of human stress you *need* to make yourself unavailable and have a long hot bath, knowing very well that the world is full of people with neither baths nor water. Things like space and time and causal necessity define so much of our belonging and our distances, whatever we *choose*.

I have argued that *alienation* is the wrong model for Christian existence, even in a politically righteous form: and I have argued that *identification* is the wrong model, since it is untruthful about what we need to be rescued from; what is left unhealed by our best efforts. How, properly, do we live as members of a church whose mission, in some sense, is to indicate, to articulate, to express this Kingdom to the world? How do we avoid neurosis and judgementalism on the one hand, because we are failing, failing, failing to budge the bloody world (including the bloody church-world) and complacency on the other, because our limits are, to a large extent, given, and need more than moral transformation? How do we find the right balance between in some sense accepting *our* humanness, with all its political and personal ironies and inconsistencies, and insisting that we must be restless and mobilised for change until the blasphemous dehumanising of our present co-existence is transformed? How do we belong and not belong?

I do not think this is a matter for ethical generalisation

at the abstract level. Christians find their vocation in a particular context. They must, here, there, now, then, do one thing or another, stand on one side or another, be caught in the crossfire, fire the crossfire. Choosing, or finding where that vocation is will always be a matter of risk and of bitter-sweetness. For as you belong, as you must, you realise that you exclude, as you must. Depending on where you find yourself, you may be whole-hearted or divided, compromised or clear in your solidarity at the local level, relaxed or struggling psychically, perplexed or confident about where you are at!

I believe that what is properly called the Church — the community of transformation which shows up our lunatic ecclesiastical structures and our broken world — exists to do several things for the world and for the Christians.

1. For the world and the Christians, it has to *register* and *confess* accurately and with the pain of solidarity, the distance there is between our existence and the Kingdom. Particularly, it has to refuse to domesticate our exclusions as having a part in God's future. In this it challenges all the belongings which define us *against* one another. So help him God, Gerry Adams is called to banquet with Ian Paisley. So help me God, I am called to banquet with both, and everything in my guts doesn't want to! I must, where I humanly belong, take sides on issues involving both. Yet I am only allowed to take sides on the basis of a recognition that who I am in Christ in some sense has to take them in. The church is to keep me alert to the complacency of my alignments, even the good ones!

2. For the world and the Christians, the Church has to *forgive* the distance and the guilt of it. This is simultaneous with confession, and is necessary if we are to stop chewing our various guilts like cud! Even our best attempts to close the distance may blunder into

utopianism or into totalitarianism, but we are released from self-preoccupation about how we are doing it wrong, into the simplicity of having love re-affirmed to us.

3. For the world and the Christians, the church has to bring into focus the closing of the distance. It cannot, given the structures of our existence, magic the distance away; but it can enact the inclusiveness of the Kingdom on various levels: liturgically, symbolically, sacramentally (flexing our imagination), prophetically/politically (challenging the excluders), microcosmically, in its own overcoming of internal alienations.

Of course, in all this I recognise that the word 'church' is irretrievably poisoned for many people by the history of Christendom and that many of our so-called churches are anti-churches. But I think our square peggery in the world can only be wholesome if we are held in some such community of truthfulness, forgiveness and promise.

As Christians, we live the tension between our rootedness in the world, which is given to us, and our rootedness in the Kingdom which is given to us, and we present them to one another. To many in society, it seems madness to want the disturbance of the Kingdom. To many in the churches it seems risky to maintain the solidarity with the world.

Our job is to be faithful to both without slithering into complacency or hating creation, or becoming holier than whatever thou. For when the new heaven and the new earth emerge from the current birth-pangs, the pegs will, I hope, fit their holes.

IX

The Churches' mission in a secularised Europe
(Conference of European Churches,
Switzerland 16-20 November 1987)

Dorothee Solle has a poem called "On being accused of being a Marxist", in which she comments, roughly, "I use the telephone daily, but no one calls me a Bellite".

The churches' relation to secularisation in Europe or elsewhere is, primarily, not "having an opinion about it", but being inextricably involved with it. It is not an option, not a dilemma for the churches to be for it or against it (like being for or against a particular reform of abortion law, or for or against a specific nuclear defence strategy).

"Could Europe have been Europe unsecularised?", "Would it have been better unsecularised?". These are abstractly hypothetical questions, inviting facilely speculative reconstruction and dangerous nostalgia for a seamlessly 'religious' world in which God, heaven, hell, etc., were axiomatic parts of the frame of reference.

The analysis of secularisation is a delicate business. It is usually done from a medieval-to-modern perspective, which concentrates on Reformation and Enlightenment, and underestimates the effective secularity of classical pre-Christian humanism. There is also a tendency in some contemporary Christian writing (eg Newbigin: *The Other Side of 1984*) to regret the rise of our post-Enlightenment axioms with their liberal optimism, their *laissez-faire* individualism and their cultural arrogance. It is of course true that we are heirs of a plundered planet in which Europe has been a primary plunderer: that the capacity for exploitation has been in part linked to technological prowess: and that technology is in part a spin-off from secularising science. Nevertheless I think we underestimate the sociological, historical, social, geographical and philosophical complexity of 'secularisation' as a phenomenon if we think we can chart it in six easy moves. I also think we have lost our theological nerve if we long to reverse it or to have reversed it; if we assume that deforestation, acid rain and the rest of our ecological crises are linked to secularisation *as such*. The work of Barth, Bultmann, Bonhoeffer, and Ronald Gregor Smith should have taken the churches past the secular/sacred polarisation and wistfulness for a more 'religious' past.

The more important critical/prophetic question seems to me to be whether Europe, as such, has a future or is culturally, socially, politically and spiritually bankrupt, in part because of its religious history.

A former colleague of mine in Edinburgh, having worked for five years in New Zealand and, having returned to Britain and Germany for six months' sabbatical, wrote of 'Europe's disintegrating culture'. To many Third World observers, the present surge of right-wing monetarist, *laissez-faire* governments, appealing to crude selfishness with the rhetoric of freedom, prolonging 'enemy' mentalities because the interests vested in these prevail against a world's starvation and hunger for peace, and continuing to treat Europe as the economic and cultural centre of the world, manifests a damnable bankruptcy. If in the world, Europe is seen as an unconfessing Empire in its death-throes, the debate about secularisation pales to insignificance, as do the denominational differences among us.

Superficially, the West is portrayed as having accepted or responded to secularisation, while the East has resisted it. This account seems to me to miss several complexities in the actual situation.

On the whole, the Western churches, while reluctantly yielding the secular entitlement to be themselves, are in fact increasingly paralysed by people just being human without reference to religion. Their identity and self-consciousness depend on being somehow or other *different* from the world, in moral achievement, in God-consciousness, in social concern, in doctrinal allegiance. This church/world polarisation has, of course, some Biblical precursors, but is in my judgement at odds with the Gospel (there is a hermeneutical issue here). I am not enough of an historian to chart exactly how and when the church *versus* world mentality became dominant, but I suspect that post-Augustinian medieval monasticism had a lot to do with it.

Eastern tradition on the other hand has in some ways a more worldly and less 'gathered' ecclesiology. The church *is* the world, but the-world-represented-in-the-fulness-of-its-future, which is to be a sharer in the life of God. It is a cosmological fact because of Christ's relationship to humanity and cosmos, not an option for people to be persuaded into. The interpenetration of our humanness — whereby any of us represents the human condition, and all are represented in the new Adam — breaks down the boundaries between holy and unholy, saints and sinners, religious and unreligious. It is suggested for instance in the whole fictional world created by Dostoevsky, or empirically in the solidarities of a Greek village which accepts the prostitute as a member, not an alien; or in the liturgical act of sharing the eucharistic bread outside the church. (This of course produces other practical/pastoral problems, eg about theocracy and dissent, or about the distance between eschatological and empirical existence.) It does not depend for its existence on a more or less growing club committed to a certain kind of piety, the achievement of a certain standard of moral or social concern, the practice of a special religious system. What makes the church matter is that it addresses the world with questions about its life and death, its freedom and hope, its catholicity even as a local community. (Of course the Orthodox churches, in practice, fail too, but their normative ecclesiology seems to me potentially more open to the secular than many Western traditions.)

I hope we are capable of recognising how much our marginalisation within Europe is *deserved*, because of our recurrent panic in the face of what we identify as secular opposition. We have not heard Bonhoeffer's challenge to explore the faith non-religiously, and that forty years on. We have not yet listened undefensively and eagerly to the bearers of our secularised culture and its values, to the artists, to the psychotherapists, to the media. If we are to share in the healing of our world's common future even, let alone to pioneer it, we must reverse our perception of 'us' as givers to needy 'them'. In Scotland, certainly, to illustrate the situation I know best, the most critical and yet cherishing appraisal of our cultural handicaps comes from poets and novelists who are explicitly atheist or agnostic, and certainly outside the church. Or, to cite a recent embarrassing example, the people to be consistently celebrated as imaginative, compassionate, and humanly open in the recent debates on AIDS have not, on the whole, been the church spokesmen, but the *not* Christianly aligned members of the Terrence Higgins Trust, a body created for the support and care of HIV and AIDS sufferers.

What then of mission in this Europe?

My sense of the present and the past makes me think that any account of the Churches' mission in Europe must purge itself of the *de facto* claim to be the bearer of the Gospel. I think we may be having the Gospel brought to us, in part from other continents and contexts, in part from our own secularised world, and in part from some of the churches (but only some) who within Eastern Europe have engaged in mutual exploration with Marxist partners of the human predicament. Are we capable of receiving it?

Christianity may have become, or be in the process of becoming, a minority faith in Europe. More significantly, one might ask whether it has become a minority faith within the churches. Have we so steadily and subtly aligned ourselves with national or state concerns, with sectarian interpretations of the faith, with exclusivist ethics and piety that we are incapable of manifesting the generosity of God to anyone? Perhaps the radical dismantling of the culture — the Christianity of our post-Constantine era — should be celebrated. The dismantling may re-expose widely, for the first time in centuries, the nerve of the evangelical question about what it means to be charged to be 'the salt of the earth'; what passion and costliness is involved in European church-belonging (cf Latin America or south-east Asia)? Can we anticipate the kingdom of God by *de iure* representation on education committees and hospital appointment boards? Are we *entitled* to land, to property, to broadcasting time? Should we really be battling for such rights?

Given this malaise within European Christianity, I find traditional aspirations to proselytise inept and offensive. If, however, we recovered in our churches the truth of *being* the Church, then proselytising would be unnecessary, for the very existence of such an 'institution' (an embodied anti-institution, refusing boundaries, refusing to outlaw sinners, resisting the bullying of the powers-that-be, even with its life) would generate for the surrounding community the amazement, horror, delight and crisis which are the dynamic of mission.

There are, I believe, some signals of such struggling to emerge from the cocoon of our European Christendom, but that already produces a problem for most of our 'churches', confronted by the need to renounce all their pride and power.

In random order, I suggest some of the signals of that Church. I know of no management procedures to produce or accelerate it, but I suspect it will be more confirmed by the world than by the 'churches' we all inhabit.

1) It will be confessing, for itself and for the world, the distance we are from the Kingdom; yet, paradoxically, it is confessing the inter-identity of Church, world and kingdom which frees us from neurotic guilt into

possibilities of relaxation and hilarity.

2) It will love the humanness around it. Instead of being nervous, defensive, moralistic, it will enjoy the specificity of the culture, temperament and history it encounters. It is out of this cherishing that the challenge of Christology and eschatology will come into focus against the possibility of this 'other's' death. It will pay particular attention to the normally uncherished; madmen, criminals, children, sexual deviants, artists, etc.

3) It will be ecumenical/catholic. Clearly there are sinister possibilities of 'pragmatic ecumenism', aimed merely at recouping losses of property, status, manpower, self-confidence. These must be distinguished from the passion against dividedness. What the latter means structurally is not clear to me, nor how to achieve it. But it will certainly mean that the mental, emotional, financial, liturgical equations between 'church' and 'denomination' will break down.

(Indeed I hope 'church*es*' becomes an obsolete word in the Christian vocabulary, even if in some form denominational diversities of emphases survive, manifesting the church.)

Yet this must not happen for reasons of liberal, *laissez-faire* politeness. It must involve passion and conflict, for the denominations emerged, at least in part, out of battles for truthfulness about the faith which were matters of life and death to people. The recapitulation of these battles, not their repetition, seems to me necessary. Yet very little happens (at least where I live) to give Christians any real sense of the scandal of our separate, and sometimes exclusive, denominational eucharists, and of the effectively sectarian character of our belonging, both in church and world. The battles of the past are merely fossilised in present habits of belonging.

4) It will enjoy theology. I find that the denominations on the whole are embarrassed by theology, partly because it has been the vehicle of so much past division, partly it has distracted people from good works (or *orthopraxis*). It also seems irretrievably remote from people's day-to-day living. While, of course, the recovery of engaged co-existence is a major gain in the global church, there is some risk, I think, of dissolving faith and apologetics into ethics. The Church needs to work at the recovery of cosmology also (not just ecological ethics as well as social). How are creation, fall and salvation understood and expressed in a world shot through with awareness of terminal environmental crisis, nuclear panic, sexual terror? What does the saving of this finite world mean?

We have increasingly isolated theologians (and they have isolated themselves) in ghettoes where they talk to one another but not to the inhabited earth. Until we recover theology as the delighted, passionate, imaginative, refreshing, terrifying, intelligent exploration of the inexhaustible God, we have no right to claim the interest or attention of the secular world.

X

Sexuality in the '90s: thinking theologically

Since Freud's articulation of the place of sexuality in human affairs, the self-consciousness of the world has been significantly nudged in new directions. Of course, in all ages and cultures, in poetry, art and drama, men and women have explored the power and centrality of sexuality in human experience. And ordinary people, in the common patterns of pairing, have lived out that centrality in celebration, pain and passion.

But since Freud and the opening up of the psychoanalytic field of human self-understanding, there has been perhaps a more systematic and sharply-focussed recognition of the role of sexuality in human growth and development. Some, of course, would criticise Freud as too determinist in his anthropology. Others, particularly feminists, find his account too genitally preoccupied and, particularly, too phallic. Yet he has clearly put on the intellectual and emotional map a recognition of how pervasive and potent a force sexuality is, from infancy onwards; and what risk of dis-ease attends its mishandling.

As an index of the shift in public consciousness, one might quote the observation of Michael Foucault in his *History of Sexuality** that, whereas traditional Christian ethics were concerned with purity, and desire was suspected as the prompting of Satan, nowadays people go to the doctor or the therapist to complain about *loss* of libido. That is to say, we assume sexual desire to be normal, natural and healthy; and its fulfilment to be a proper aspiration and a primary enrichment of human life.

Apart from, or along with, this major shift of attitude, we inherit in the nineties all the more specific social developments

* A paper given to Wooster College, Ohio, USA, September 1990

in relation to medical technology, cultural patterns, ideological movement and genetic research. The details of those need more detailed sociological attention than I can give, but I indicate the range of factors by citing four: (i) the progressive refinement of contraceptive techniques; (ii) several decades of mixed-sex campus proximity; (iii) the re-emergence of feminism as a major social force; (iv) accumulating medical evidence on the involuntary character of sexual orientation.

Until very recently, the impact of such convergent elements was a relaxing of taboos which had been the 'official' sexual ethic of a society at least nominally Christian. (The 'Christian West' may be now a fiction, but it has till recently been a fiction significant for purposes of social control.) One British survey, issued in 1989 suggested that some 80% of British young adults have some active sexual relationship without being married, or even intending marriage; and increasingly with no sense of furtiveness or guilt. In the last decade the trend has stopped rising, apparently in direct relation to the AIDS risk; but such change is associated with fear and prudence, rather than with any *moral* re-appraisal of the intrinsic rightness or wrongness of pre-marital sex. The legalising of same-sex relationships, and the often costly campaigning of Gay Rights activists, has created at least the beginning of social recognition that there are diverse and plural modes of sexual partnership. The pressures towards furtiveness and alienation, however, may be mounting again, as the scapegoating of gay men and women increases in some quarters in relation to the threat of AIDS.

Among the young, almost universally outside the churches (and to some extent within them I suspect), the criteria of a good relationship, sexual or not, would seem to be such things as integrity, loyalty, candour, mutual respect, enhanced communication, shared commitment about the character of the relationship, and so on. Within that horizon, duration or permanence or physical sexual activity may be regarded as variables rather than as absolutes.

The churches meanwhile, by and large, wrestle uneasily with questions in this area. Most register the shifts in sexual pattern with some consternation, maintaining at the official level that the norm remains the traditional one, that heterosexual monogamous marriage is the only divinely sanctioned context for sexual activity. Premarital, extra-marital, post-marital or homosexual activism is, with various pitches of pastoral tone, regretted or deplored. A few voices, of whom I suppose the best-known would be the American bishop, Jack Spong, challenge received orthodoxy with public boldness. But the commoner situation, if my experience at the American Episcopal Bishops' Conference in September 1990 is anything to go by, is that many have strong private liberal convictions and will exercise them with discretion, but wish to avoid the polarising backlash likely to be provoked in church circles by the public sanctioning of gay or extramarital sex.

Acknowledgement of ethical diversity in this area, far less acceptance of it, is patchy in Christian circles: and it seems that the subject is once again seen as a painful nettle, to be grasped only with very thick gloves on!

If all that can stand as a thumbnail sketch of where we started the nineties, I want now to explore the question whether Christian Theology has any distinctive response to make in the present socio-cultural context, any particular appraisal of sexuality, any criteria of 'good' and 'bad' relationships, which is neither mere borrowing from the sanity of post-Freudian humanism, nor the atavistic hurling of Biblical rocks at people struggling to be truthful in this area. How do the diverse sources of Christian theology in experience, scripture, tradition, reason and the imagination of love converge or diverge on sexuality issues? How do we handle theologically the *de facto* pluralism of contemporary Christian conviction? Do we see it as sinister proof that something has gone far wrong? Or can we find creativity, albeit painful creativity, in the present unfinished conversation?

It is in commitment to the latter hope that I offer the following contribution.

While sexual *ethics* have featured high on church agendas past and present, less attention has been give to the place of sexuality in what might be called 'Theological Anthropology'. Clearly, at the level of human experience, sexuality is a basic dimension — some would say *the* basic dimension — of our humanness. But what is our sexuality before God? Is our distinctiveness, our particularity, our irreplaceability as persons to God and to one another bound up with our determinate sexual embodiedness?

The conviction suggested by the first Creation myth in Genesis, carried somewhat uneasily for tracts of Christian teaching, and at times utterly lost, is that our being male and female is part of the good and specific end-intent of God's creation, our paradisal invitation. Indeed, the parallelism of Genesis 1:27 "God made man in his own image, made him in the image of God. Man and woman both, he created them" almost seems to allow for the possibility that our sexual differentiation and complementarity in some way reflects God's being. But what then does this mean if God is sexless or a-sexual, "without parts and passions" as in Judaeo-Christian tradition 'he' classically and ironically is? For sexuality is very much bound up with parts and passions, with physiology, biology, psychology. If sexuality belongs exclusively to the realm of creation, how do we link our ultimate self-identification in relation to God? And if we cannot so link it — if we say, in effect, that our sexuality has no bearing on our existence in 'redemption' — are we not very deeply split about the core of our faith-identity and the core of our human selves?

When one moves beyond the physiological, chromosomal differentiations of body structure and hormonal characteristics which most obviously identify people as male and female, it seems to me that any definition of maleness and femaleness is tantalisingly elusive. What Jung called 'masculine' and 'feminine' characteristics, intelligence/intuition, thought/feeling, activity/passivity, etc., now seem questionably stereotyped. As soon as you move from generic to particular accounts of people, and recognise the intricate interweaving of aggression, tenderness, critical intelligence, intuition in any of us, it becomes a somewhat arbitrary matter of stipulation to call some aspects *animus* and others *anima*. Much of that classification, like the labelling of people as 'effeminate men' or 'mannish women' is deeply questionable, as being in large measure the construct of social mythology and cultural policy rather than self-evident data. Of course, chromosome research may turn out to be much more precise than hitherto about ranges of standard psycho-somatic sexual correlates: but so far, it seems to me, there is more dogma than data about *essential* gender-linked characteristics. And the mystery of our particularity in all areas, including the sexual, transcends generic description.

The clue, then, in understanding sexuality in theological terms, must lie in some understanding of how the dynamism of sexual interaction is significant for our *personal*, distinctive identity. There are, of course, aspects of sexuality which are significantly *im*personal. Cupid is blind. All our images of sexual magnetism, of random or orgiastic attraction testify to that (and provide one reason why the Christian Church felt it had to do battle with Pan and Bacchus). But there are also ways in which sexual encounter can open up for us aspects of what freedom and communion are about, and can thus image, however partially, encounter with the personhood of God.

i) Sexuality aspires to *ecstasy*. It does not always make it, but at its best it is a paradigm of being taken out of oneself, of being able to let go, of being delimited, of joy

107

ii)   Sexuality involves coming to terms with the *otherness* of any other. This, of course, has some generic components. For a woman, to explore any man's body is to explore something in some ways familiar, in some ways 'other', and *vice versa*. And this is also true in same-sex relationships. But as those with multiple sexual experiences testify, knowing this person's body is different from knowing that one's body (even if you are familiar with the *generic* sexual characteristics involved). It looks as if people have varying registers of sensitivity here. Just as some people register the pitch of voices while others are tone-deaf, so some people register sexually with immensely specific precision, while others have much less delicate apprehensions, and might as well, in Arthur Miller's horrendous image, "screw inside paper sacks with holes in them"! Personal and impersonal sexuality may also have to do with this register of the particularity of the other

iii) Sexuality, when not reduced to genital sensation, is a mode of intense and total vulnerability, where one is quite exposed. For instance, possessiveness, manipulation, greed, boredom, generosity, anger, relaxation, self-preoccupation, zest, imagination, tiredness, etc., become palpable and transparent

iv)   Sexuality is a focus of truthfulness about our involvement in the birth-death continuum with which we are bound up in the realm of biological process. Here, where we are most preciously flesh to one another, we are also most aware of our fragility. The pathos of sexuality, as well as the elation of it, is multiply attested.

If sexuality can be a vehicle of ecstasy, of recognition of otherness, of transparency and of truthful vulnerability, then it seems to me that it deserves to be called 'good', not just in the relatively low-key sense of "what most people find agreeable and desirable", but also in the theologically tough sense of "that which belongs, or contributes, to our wholeness, our well-being before God and with one another".

It does not, however, contribute automatically or necessarily. There are modes of sexuality which are exploitative; which ignore or even violate the 'otherness' of another; which mask those involved rather than disclosing them; which never move beyond the projection of one self onto another. And these are possible modes even within the technically sanctioned sexual relationships which traditional Christian ethics allow. Conversely, the traditionally condemned relationships may manifest the four characteristics suggested as imaging encounter with God.

If we are to approach Christian ethical articulation about sexuality it is, I suggest, more important to clarify these positive and negative *modes* of sexual involvement than to concentrate on particular acts, or classes of acts (like 'fornication' or 'adultery'). There may, of course, be likely connections. It may be hard-to-impossible for someone involved in an adulterous relationship to retain transparency, or respect for both 'others'. But this does not vitiate the demand in principle for a shift to the qualitative appraisal of sexuality, rather than the confessionally quantitative approach. (When? How often? With whom?)

Thus the relative badness or goodness of specific forms of sexual behaviour may depend more on their modality than on formal circumstances. The important question will not be, for instance, whether a young person has slept with more than one person, but whether their sexual exploration and self-exploration is undertaken with callousness or tenderness, with candour or evasiveness, in growing self-knowledge or floundering in alien roles, drifting or identifying firm markers towards sexual maturity.

In the same way, the polarising of homosexual relationships as intrinsically bad and heterosexual ones as intrinsically good (the conventional and traditional Christian position) must be re-evaluated, not because all notions of good and bad are being relativised and abandoned but because 'good' needs to be assessed in terms of a relationship's capacity to be a vehicle of the kind of love-in-freedom which images God's own life. And that wind, too, "blows where it listeth".

There are, however, for many devout Christians, still massive worries about Scripture and/or Church tradition in relation to all this. It looks to them like outright war between the authoritative sources of the past and the so-called wisdom of secular culture or liberal Christian ethics. They shudder at the challenge of Don Cupitt's *New Christian Ethics* where he writes:

> A modern Christian ethic can only be had if we utterly forget pre-Enlightenment Christianity ... We can today be Christians only at the price of saying there wasn't any Christianity to speak of before the later eighteenth century, and certainly none of any interest or relevance to us. The earlier religion was ... otherworldly, radically anti-human and anti-life ... Our ethic will be an ethic of the flesh, an ethic of human feeling, an ethic of libido and of being true to the life energy in us!

Well, if that is the price of being modern Christians, say many, it is too high. Better the constraints of an orthodox morality than the abandonment of so much Christian heritage!

I am quite convinced that this is a false antithesis; that if we wrestle with our Christian past with all the energy and courtesy and openness and determination we would wish to bring to encounters in the Christian present, we will not find it an either/or between their sense of life and ours. We will find, then *and* now, conflicts about where authority lies, about the freedom to re-interpret Scripture, about the locus of present revelation, about who has the Spirit, about who should be excluded from Christian community. The key question is not whether such diversity occurs, and has occurred right back to the Scriptural roots of Christian faith; I am sure it does and has. The key question is whether the churches can only view that diversity with dismay, and retreat from it behind battlements of impregnable authority. Or whether they can find, in the very wrestling for truth and meaning, an inviting God who calls us to explore the future with zest. This does not mean abandoning, or ignoring or cursing the past, but making it part of the unfinished, unboundaried conversation with present and future to which human history, human culture, human faith all belong. To be open to that under God is not culture-relativism. It is eschatological absolutism. You do not know who you are till you see who you will be! So you must keep wrestling with everything.

Let me be, however, a little more precise, for a general exhortation to wrestle well may not be of much supportive value to communities which are already exhausted with such wrestling, and hardly know how to get out of the various clichés which keep recurring: "It's natural, but is it right? It must be right if it's natural!" "It can't be right; Scripture's against it." "So much the worse for Scripture!" "Godless atheist!" "Fundamentalist idiot!" Write your own cliché!

There are three primary areas where, I think, we need to do more delicate theological work than has been done, although all I can do here is to indicate an agenda. I hope that even the articulation of that might be a tiny contribution to the present church debate, which actually seems to me handicapped by its theological naiveté, as well as by its incapacity to look for Christ in the strangeness of the other.

Firstly, the understanding of nature as created and fallen. The traditions of the Church in relation to sexuality have not been good. From an opening statement in Genesis myth which appears to be celebratory, Western Europe at least has spent centuries feeling it had to contest paganism by deploring, subduing and sometimes crucifying nature. For all its early battles with Gnosticism, Christianity has actually 'out-gnosticked' the gnostics at times in its loathing of flesh, and in its placing of nature as a sinister, potentially lethal environment, matched by a correspondingly lethal disposition to sin which is our 'inner nature'. Formal Roman Catholic theology has always said that God perfects nature rather than abolishes it. But on the ground, and particularly in the bed, that 'perfecting' has meant stopping doing what *actually* comes naturally because it is 'unnatural'; and a very restrictive normative use of the word 'natural' has throttled the apparent permissiveness of 'follow Nature'. Sex at the wrong time in the wrong place with the wrong person or the wrong bit of the body (and that, notoriously, has sometimes meant everything except missionary-position penetration by a monogamous heterosexual couple) is redefined as 'unnatural'.

I am not opposed *in principle* to words like 'natural' taking on such shifts of meaning: it seems to me indeed, that that would be like opposing the tide, for language evolves in the freedom of cultural shifts, and at its richest is full of such changes and redirections of meaning. But we do need to register with some retrospective delicacy what the shifts have been, especially when people are baffled, and even wounded by the clash of meanings. Many people who feel quite dehumanised by Church denunciation of their behaviour as 'unnatural', (which they recognise as a boo-word) might be marginally comforted to hear the same church saying: "Oh, we know it's *absolutely* natural in *your* sense of 'coming from overwhelming and unsought-for instincts'. That's our problem with it!".

But more often, the response of the unchurched or the sexual counter-culture in the church is to defend and exalt nature-as-it-comes, with the often-explicit premises that "whatever is, is right". God set it up. It is here. It is good. It must, therefore, be OK. This is, perhaps, the commonest argument used in Gay Christian circles, and because we are, many of us, so clear that welcome and celebration are long overdue to this abused minority, we tend to turn a blind eye to the quality of the argument; since, in any case, the violence of their earlier rejection and exclusion from community and church is rarely a matter of the head but of deeper homophobia.

The defence of any sexual act or orientation as natural is, of course, part of a larger re-appraisal of the natural which is going on in our culture. Nature is big business. If one dishwasher is more 'natural' than another, it sells. Organic bread, wine, cheese adorn the tables of the rich at four times the cost of the same unadulterated food on the tables of peasants. We are so aware of the exploitative abuse of the environment, the risks of the plastic culture, the connections between advanced technology and the potential for global disaster that, almost as an act of atonement, of contrition, we are recycling like mad, planting wildlife gardens, creating health-food booms and hoping that we can retrieve an equilibrium where we hear and follow nature, rather than dominate it.

It seems to me that we must, at this historico-cultural juncture, beware of a new idolatry about nature. Respect, maybe even reverence, yes. Cherishing, cradling, healing if we can, the wounds of our own greed and carelessness, yes. But I think we cannot buy the kind of cosmological Toryism of Alexander Pope's Essay on Man, "Whatever is, is right".

What I am pleading for is a new exploration of the doctrine of the Fall, especially as it relates to the natural and cosmic dimensions of our existence. (On the socio-political dimensions we are, by contrast, over-exposed to self-consciousness about the mess.) For when we have waded back through the swamps of centuries of Christian psychopathology about sex, flesh and nature, I believe we find a realism and clarity about our fragility which we have well-nigh lost in our Pelagian, managerial, self-improving ethics. And that realism and clarity properly counters the utopian idealising of sexuality as what constitutes our lives as human beings. For the core of the Greek Patristic appraisal of sexuality, before salacious morbidity became the commoner theological response, was surely that our sexuality is embedded existentially in the whole process of birth *and* death. We cannot isolate the bio-genetic-cellular-muscular processes of love-making either from their potential for birth or from their potential towards death. (Of course, we can play around with the time-scales a bit, given contraceptives, aerobics classes and dietary regimes; but basically, a-morally, we cannot isolate the processes of sexuality, birthing and nurture from the biological cycle of decay and death.) This means that any talk of sexuality as 'life-enhancing', true as it is at the psychological level, is a cop-out at the level of ontology from the pathos of our ending.

It is the isolation of sexuality from all the other areas of ambivalence in our embodied existence that makes it excessively morbid to dwell on. Eating feeds us and also feeds the processes of our dying. Breathing is vital, but poisons the air. The management of the earth produces life-giving resources, but simultaneously exhausts others. Nor is this mere ethics about *better* farming, *better* eating, *better* ecological care, the renunciation of nasty capitalist greed. Even our best, most subtle, most loving, indeed finest acts as embodied beings are caught in this pathos of finitude. There is a New Zealand poet, Arthur Baysting, who writes on this point:

> Yes, I agree,
> there's been too much
> exploitation of resources
> but
> I like music
> and that piano
> was once
> trees and rocks
> and elephants.

How often do we want, need to be with two people at the same time but have been unable to do it because of separating space and time? How often have we had all the desire in the world to do something crying to be done and not been able to because of the frailty of nerve and bone and gut?

It is no gnostic dualism, but the frustration of our love and freedom which happen time and time again which makes us say, "This sweet earth, this sweet flesh, which mediate to us so much of our communion, also frustrate it, and very often simultaneously". And this applies also to sexuality. Indeed it is almost commonplace in the often-recorded melancholy of post-coital experience that there is such woe in the unsustainability of sexual exhilaration as to be pain.

It is perhaps, especially for the nineties, important for us to recover the irony of how 'normal' sexuality, even 'normal' heterosexual monogamous sexuality is embedded in the life-death continuum, because that relates us to rather than dissociating us from the community which is currently facing, in a telescoped and graphic way, the link between sexuality and death. It is, sickeningly, the delight of some moralists and sensationalists to create links between 'abnormal' sex and the 'abnormal' pathology of HIV+ infection, which charges every new sexual encounter with a new edge of menace. We might better combat the marginalising and scapegoating of people living with AIDS if we were merely candid about all sexuality's inextricable involvement in the processes of our mortality.

Secondly, if the Theology of Nature needs attention, so does what I might call the Theology of Ethics. Ethics we all know; and ethics is what theological discussion of sexuality usually reduces to, partly because most of us actually find it an area of such explosive potential in ourselves that urgent questions about how to handle it are nearly always there. I suspect that in fact in all societies, many of the 'rules' in the area of sexuality emerge from society's panic, which is ours writ large, at the potency and potential chaos of sexual impulse, and from the need for control and regulation both in relation to the rearing of children and to the disposal of land and property. When I speak of the Theology of Ethics, I do not mean the what-are-we-to-do questions: should I sleep with this person at point X? Should I give this job to this person knowing his/her sexual orientation? How should I respond to someone wanting to quit a marriage of such and such characteristics? These are, of course, burning existential questions. But I think we need to spend more time on what is called in theology the relationship between 'eschatology' and 'ethics': that is, what sort of connections are there between our sense or vision of the Kingdom of God and what we do, here and now, about this or that?

My reading of the Kingdom of God is of a community of love and freedom in which there will be no constraint, no conditionality and no exclusion from above. It does not depend on who you are, what you have achieved, what you have failed in, that you are loved. Your particularity of being, what the Greeks would have called 'form' and the New Testament 'body', is irreplaceably precious. And being 'made fit' for the Kingdom is to do with learning to live with delight, prodigally and without limits, in that mutuality of preciousness with whatever other we meet. Most of us, unfortunately, go into shock or nervous breakdown if we have to cope with mutuality in relation to more than two and a half relationships! Earth cannot cope with eternal triangles, let alone eternal polygons!

Some early Christian sects said: "Well, we live anticipating heaven and unbound by earth. Let us have holy promiscuity". And they did, but were excommunicated by orthodoxy.

Much more commonly, the churches have said that if you try to turn the Kingdom into ethics, you get into a mess. Here on earth we need constraint, order, structures which recognise and control our imperfectness. It is utopian to offer men and women the freedom of heaven. For earth, one needs

116

earthbound ethics; and sane social experience shows that all communities without strict controls on sexual behaviour reap disaster.

It is possibly a matter of disposition, need and training, rather than of argument, where one's heart and head lie on this. I have only one overriding conviction. If we go for the ethics, or non-ethics of heaven, we must be prepared for disaster on earth: for the world cannot in its present natural structures tolerate the freedom of heaven, and it will need, seek, be bound to crucify any bearer of such freedom, recognising the death-threat to its own normality.

If we go for the ethics of earth, we will literally manage better. There will be less chaos: society will know roughly where it stands: we will be responsible; able to identify and penalise deviants from our social norms. But we dare not identify God with these norms. For if there is one person on earth who is, by such ethics, devalued, dehumanised, demonised or disqualified from the conversation towards truth, whether that be on grounds of sexual behaviour or any other, then I believe we lie, and possibly blaspheme. We certainly fail to be bearers of good news. For as black hole is to star (we are invited to hope), the generosity of God encompasses and sustains and surpasses our need for one another as it transforms beyond our wildest dreams the ecstasy of the earth.

The *third* area is, not surprisingly, in hermeneutics. What are we to do about all the verses from Leviticus, Romans, Corinthians, etc., which, plain as a pikestaff, denounce homosexuality, for instance, as well as the heterosexual sins of fornication, adultery, etc? The secular world can say "Stuff Scripture! Irrelevant to our culture!" But what does the Church have to say? For many, of course, there is no problem except the devout wrestling to be obedient: if Scripture says it, it is right, true, absolute, normative.

It is those Christians on the middle ground who have not

117

yet done well enough in articulating a hermeneutic: those who believe that Scripture is a not-dispensable primary reference-point for the Church as it wrestles with the living God, and yet do not believe that it has to be treated as a norm of undifferentiated and uniform prescriptiveness for all times and places.

Again, argument here can only be sketchy but must, I believe, involve candour rather than furtiveness about the difficulties. In particular, the following elements have to be fed into any discussion:

i)   Once Scripture is stratified into the time-contexts and culture-contexts of its sources, we can in fact detect quite matter-of-fact recognition of sexual practices which later tradition judges as unacceptable (eg concubinage, surrogacy, homosexuality (David and Jonathan?), prostitution (Rahab).

ii) The main horror of Jewish and early Judaeo-Christian contexts at these sexual practices was their contemporary status as part of *pagan* practice, especially the nature religions. If it is *not* nature-worship but the exploring of loving, caring relationship under the generosity of the ecstatic, vulnerable, truthful God which is the interiority of the sexual relationship, the focus is quite different.

iii) What we know about biological and physiological nature was unknown throughout the whole scriptural period. Ethical dogma based on ignorance of the (increasingly established) data is as obscurantist as cosmological dogma based on pre-Copernican astronomy.

iv) It is at least debatable that sexual mores belong as much to social mores which scriptural writings take for granted (cf slavery) as to 'timeless truths' about human nature, ie the speculative, but important and inescapable, question is not "Did Paul speak against homosexuality?" (answer 'Yes'), but "If Paul were engaging in the twentieth century debate, would he be speaking against it?''. The fact that we cannot cross-question Paul across the centuries does not remove the leverage of the question. One can, for instance, see the debate as a twentieth century 'circumcision' issue, a Christ and culture question in which the deeper, underlying Pauline stance may be argued to be the radical one. That it could not be in first century Corinth was due to the accidental, contextual rooting of homosexuality in paganism, which was really Paul's target.

v) Reformation hermeneutics are not in fact fundamentalist, though they are often treated as being so. Luther's freedom to denounce James as "a right strawy epistle'', the various accounts of how the Spirit discriminates, quickens and directs the Church in its handling of the text, and the precedents of Reformed exegesis (Mary Slessor: "Naw, naw, Paul, this winna' dae!'') all allow more of a dialectical response to what a given text says than many allow today.

vi) If, in addition, we consider the diversity of 'faithful' exegesis in such hermeneutical contexts as Liberation Theology or Feminism, we have to recognise how much *probability* there is that our own hermeneutical assumptions are as much brought to Scripture as given by it, and are liable to be tinged with the moral, sociological colour of our own structures of ethical and political control, not to speak of our own corporate psychopathologies.

None of this involves saying that sexuality is a matter of *laissez-faire* self-determination. That is a possible and common secular position, but not that of this essay. Rather I am arguing for a hermeneutic of eschatological generosity which carries its own criteria of judgement.

XI

"Thy Kingdom come"
A conversation on mission

Snarl   We meet again, Swither*. This latest statement of yours on mission is another example of contemporary theological dithering. You're trying to reconcile the embarrassing imperatives of an authoritarian tradition with the civilised politeness of a European liberal. It can't be done.

Swither   That's not what I'm trying to do. The tension seems to me to occur within the Gospel itself. On the one hand you have a church ardent to share its excitement about Christ with everyone. On the other hand you have the substantial content of the good news — a God who moves so delicately among men that he wouldn't pressurise a bending reed. You can't in the context of such a God go bullying men to abandon their cultural roots and become Christian overnight.

Snarl   Well, that's what seemed to happen when the church had its theological nerve. After all, if you really believe people are lost without the gospel, it's surely a matter of some urgency to put them right. And if you don't believe they're lost without us, there's no real gospel to preach is there, just a cultural optional extra?

Swither   I think that's rather a crude alternative. As I understand it, people would have been 'lost', as you

---

* These characters were sparring partners in the concluding chapter of *The Nature of Belief*, Sheldon Press, 1976

graphically put it, without Christ: but since his decisive intervention in the world's life, to be 'lost' is not possible. The Church's job is to represent and communicate the hope which already belongs to the whole world in virtue of Christ's identification with it.

Snarl   What's that supposed to mean? Look at the statistics of disintegration around. Look at the millions of children born to premature death. Look at the ecological projections. Look at the panic-stricken, cut-throat world. What kind of hope is all that?

Swither   I know, I know. It's not a publicly observable, testable hope, and never has been. No one could prove Jesus beat death in terms that were objectively certain. The dying went on. Divided and tangled and frustrated human relationships went on. There was no conclusive glory. And yet there was a new community entirely living out of its hopes that these familiar conditions of existence were really the past of the world. Now it was invited to a new future, prefigured symbolically or sacramentally by the church. There, death was *impotent* to intimidate people into separateness and aggression. They died for one another. What was technically 'theirs' was effectively everyone's. They expected the future to consolidate their new condition of being so that the kingdom would be manifest to all the world.

Snarl   Come off it! Such a starry-eyed, Lukan picture! I grant you they expected some kind of cosmic big bang for a few decades, and thought everything would change, but it never came. So, like most institutions, they had to find a rationale for their own existence, and did it in terms of mission. The breathing space before the eschaton (receding with every new generation further towards vanishing point) was suddenly re-interpreted to the convenience of all concerned as the age of the Church, the time when the good news could be preached to all the world. But it actually turned in to a first-rate takeover of secular empire-building, and the real end was to win wealth and influence for the church itself. Now the chance of that objective is clearly going the way of the eschaton, and the church is desperately scrabbling to find a new role in terms of 'in' moral issues or political alignments. But it has nothing distinctive to offer.

Swither   I wonder if it hasn't. Of course it must recognise its own muddy history, and confess the confusion between its own self-interest and the interest of the Kingdom, but that is no disproof of its hope. The Gospel is not easy magic. It is an invitation to struggle, even to die, in the conviction that some kinds of living are more like dying, and some kinds of dying more like living. And there *have* been moments when the church has stood for that, however 'confessingly': times when it has, for the sake of the kingdom, been willing to lay down its life. That is what we are called to do now; not talk, but live in the service of a future which is worth any cost, against the present of unfreedom or injustice or lovelessness. That's how we implement the mission of "the man for others".

Snarl   That's no gospel! That's humanitarian social work!

Swither   But surely they can't be divided. People are whole beings, a complex reality embedded in a context which defines our identity. If we have good news for the world, it must address us where we are, in context. It must be concrete. Only some kind of Greek or medieval fiction can address our souls about their wellbeing as if they were detachable from our whole embodiedness in a network of structured and unstructured involvements.

Snarl   Well, if I read the Gospel aright, none of that 'network' makes 'the real us'. Who we are is 'hid with God in Christ'? You said yourself that the church believed it already manifested the Kingdom, freed from worldly care. But now you're interpreting its good news in terms of highly worldly messages about having enough to eat, and political liberation and wellbeing which is very definitely a thing of this world. That may all be humanly worthwhile, but stop pretending it's a distinctive gospel.

Swither   I don't think the Gospel *equates* worldly wellbeing with the kingdom of God either, because such things are achievable by skill in the world's power-games, by learning how to operate within its structures. Certainly the Gospel is that there will be/are new structures, discontinuous with the present ones to some extent, not evolving from them, not manageable, not vulnerable to death and isolation and the awful transience of things. But some of the relative freedoms we encounter even in this world's terms may at least be analogues for the unrestricted freedom of being for which we long and hope. And if it's a freedom won by the rich and powerful willingly identifying with the poor

123

and dispossessed, then it already has the quality of strangeness which signals its eschatological significance.

Snarl   Rubbish! It signals not uncommon human generosity and commoner human common-sense that if you leave disaster spreading you may get sucked into it in the long run! Why dress it up in theological language? Anyway, this 'alternative structures' stuff is sheer verbal fantasy, a back-to-the-wall gambit to label some distinctive identity. But why should it be good news to anyone that there's an alternative world? It's here we belong, here we have our joys and sorrows. We'd certainly all like a bit more of the joy side, but it's not going to cheer us up to be told to invest ahead in some speculative and incoherent 'alternative future'.

Swither   It's not speculative. If people scrutinise their existence truthfully, it has radically unsatisfactory features which they can't eliminate by any socio-political strategy. It has death. It has spatio-temporal structures which frustrate meeting at all sorts of critical junctures. It has sheer exhaustibility built in, which means that even the most open and generous person can only take so much, physically and psychically. None of it is culpable moral failure. It's what they used to call the pathos of finitude.

Snarl   And what's *your* good news? That it's not really finite? That God is going to swoop down one fine Monday morning to stop the rot, pick the dead out of their graves and translate us all to angelic realms where we can be in two places at once? Come off it! You're not, mercifully, going to get twentieth century people going back to that sort of spiritual fantasy.

124

Swither   You caricature, as always. But the church affirms
that God did stop the rot, precisely and specifically
in the person of Christ. When they try to say how
he was recognisably himself, in spite of having
died, they can't do it in terms of existing structures
of being. But it seemed that his presence with one
person no longer necessitated his absence from
another. And whatever became of the local body
of the dead Jesus of Nazareth, his concrete
resurrection presence was in and with the
community he sent to be his new manifestation in
the world. So we talk in baptism of achieving a new
identity through the mutuality of his being and
ours, and of that being sustained in the eucharistic
'communion of saints', where we already taste the
new existence of the Kingdom.

Snarl   Enthusiastic mumbo-jumbo! You may symbolise
or image some incredible never-never-land, but you
are in no way empirically altered. In church or out,
you are the same disintegrating people, and there
isn't the least glimmer of you transcending the
limits of our normally structured existence.

Swither   Again, you're looking for public magic. But the
sheer fact that, in the face of all the human
structures of the world, of sociological co-ordinates
which threaten to define it, the church affirms its
own identity in quite different terms — that is itself
a strangeness which invites attention. By representing the equal strangeness of the historical
and living Christ to men and women, the church
then offers a challenge to people's obvious and
learned confidence as to who they are. It says "Are
you really content with an ultimately self-contained,
isolated existence, in which you will be picked off

sooner or later by sniping death, or are you interested in a new structure of existence where you are no longer an atomistic fragment, but reintegrated with the life of God himself?".

Snarl Any religion worth its salt says that, some more economically and without all this palaver about mediation. Hinduism tells people that they are only seemingly separate, but really are all one with Brahman. Every faith there is offers ultimate wellbeing. So why not let everyone find their own way to the transcendent, and stop this absurd insistence on the Christian thing being unique?

Swither Because I'm not at all sure it *is* the same thing they all say. For instance, it seems to me as if Hinduism and Buddhism encouraged people away from the concreteness of their embodied history to believe in a timeless, spaceless, undifferentiated reality.

Snarl Weren't you doing that a minute ago with all that ranting about transformed structures and spatio-temporal reality?

Swither No, transforming isn't abolishing. The New Testament affirms together continuity *and* discontinuity, but never that our specific, historical particularity is illusory. We are sustained in our distinctiveness; there is no blurring of one self into another. But we are no longer isolable in our particularities, but freely interdependent. Being in Christ doesn't mean me not being me, nor you not you. But it does mean I can no longer be me without you.

Snarl I haven't a clue what that means, except that it

126

sounds like a disgusting loss of individual autonomy. But even suppose I take you seriously, tell me, did Christ do whatever he did just for those in the church, or for the world as a whole?

Swither   For the world. At least he made the new life a possibility for the world. But, like God, he never acts coercively. So the actualising of the possibility involves human participatory freedom. The church is the community of those who celebrate the possibility, and therefore actualise it.

Snarl   But millions must get excited at the idea of overcoming death and separation. They don't need to be anywhere near the empirical church. Are they not already actually related to your promising Christ? Why need they be involved in historical Christianity? Can't God communicate with them independently? Can't his love find better indigenous idioms in other cultures? Why do you want to complicate things by making them swallow Christian culture?

Swither   I don't think Christianity's a culture: it's an anti-culture. It uproots people from identification with any particular place or world-view.

Snarl   But you just said "We are sustained in our distinctiveness". You're playing tricks again!

Swither   No, we've a double identity. One is our natural context which we affirm, albeit critically, in the light of the other. The other is our identity in relation to Christ, the catholic or representative person who belongs to no specific culture.

Snarl	Nonsense. He was a first century Palestinian Jew. And anyway, your description sounds positively schizoid — though I suppose that's not surprising after all Paul's imagery of the New Adam fighting the Old Adam.
Swither	Of course Jesus was a Jew, but Judaism couldn't contain him. He disrupted it as he disrupts any culture. But that does not mean he was schizoid. If you criticise your own limits for the sake of a larger humanness, you can live quite creatively out of that tension. Luther called it *'simul iustus et peccator'* (at the same time, righteous and sinner). Barth called it 'dialectically negated and affirmed'. The New Testament calls it 'loved and judged'. And that is why the church must confront any culture, including its own sociological 'home base'. It is not there for the ordinary human exchange of another culture, with all the creative and destructive potential of that. It's to face every given culture with the anti-culture of the Kingdom of God.
Snarl	My God, you're arrogant! I can see I was wrong to accuse you of departing from authoritarian tradition. You're as much a proselytiser as anyone I've met. All that stuff earlier on about not bullying people to abandon their cultural roots was so much claptrap. You may have the odd tactical disagreement with soap-box evangelicals, but you've no real difference in aim or motive. You may prefer to attract attention by aligning with socio-political causes, preach more discreetly, but by Jove, you're out to get them just the same!
Swither	No, I meant what I said. I do believe they can't find freedom or salvation out of their cultural

roots, any more than we can. But I deplore any attempt to put them under pressure. And with the history of Christendom so ambiguously behind us, I wonder whether the church's very presence isn't bound to be a pressure in some places. After all, if we were faithful in imagining the kingdom where we are, the world would presumably come galloping with questions. The fact that we have to set out to *go* anywhere is a sign of how badly we *are*. It's different being invited, but going uninvited to tell people anything makes me very uneasy.

Snarl   But you said yourself, your existence is going to be ambiguous anyway, since you can't fly out of your pre-eschatological sin. So you *must* speak to clarify the ambiguity.

Swither   I don't know. The one thing I want the church to offer the world is a glimpse of what free existence would really be like. But under the conditions of existence I think that means *either* that church and Christians are faithful and get clobbered by the world, *or* they are unfaithful and live as a 'confessing church'. Either way, there's a kind of irony in witnessing to freedom by any kind of insistent presence, especially in view of our past. Perhaps people might have more freedom to find us in our absence.

Snarl   What on earth does that mean?

Swither   Well, suppose, in a Kierkegaardian fashion, I hoped you might love me, or come to. If I constantly hovered around you, plied you with gifts, entertained you, gratified your desires, I could not know, nor could you, whether you accepted my presence out of habit, or from need which I had created, or in real freedom. If, on the other hand, I distance myself unobtrusively enough not to be simply bullying you by letting you see how dreadfully you miss me if I withdraw abruptly — if, say, I withdraw for some time, when your attention is diverted elsewhere for a sustained period — then the question really arises whether you want me; whether, for instance, you would bother to come looking for me in a far country, or sell all you have to find me. Otherwise my existence is really a matter of ultimate indifference to you. Similarly, if the church really trusted itself as the bearer of God's love, it would perhaps be less insistent about how valuable its presence is everywhere.

Snarl   That sounds absolutely perverse to me. How are they even to be aware of you if you don't put yourself empirically where they are?

Swither   How are we aware of God who doesn't appear empirically where we are? Maybe by love and by longing. Of course, we can be present as fellow-humans, doing all the co-operative things that belong to the fabric of our co-humanity, helping one another in this or that political, economic, social or emotional distress (and in the process, incidentally, clarifying the truth about the limits and frustrations of that good mutuality). But we don't do that as church, as the signal of the kingdom.

Snarl   Isn't there a grotesque division between your humanness and your existence as church? You can be humanly there, but as church you must be absent! That's schizoid again. Anyway, you can't love what's not there.

Swither Can't you? Then how did creation happen?

Snarl Oh, for goodness sake, come back to solid earth! What you've just said sounds like a classic pietist defence of Christian inertia. The apostles didn't sit in Jerusalem waiting for their absence to be felt. They went out, as you put it, 'on the aggressive', thrusting Christ in front of people. What use is a church that *does* nothing for the world or the kingdom of God? You have to work for it: it won't come by waiting. When the apostles prayed 'Thy kingdom come', they jolly well went out simultaneously campaigning for it.

Swither Yes, but I'm not sure we can construe their campaigning in terms of our natural activisms. I mean prayer, for instance, in the world's terms is *in*action: but precisely because it's offering the world to the action of God's freedom, not equitable with our impact on it in the course of business, it is eschatological action. And all these 'unnatural' things like fasting or poverty or chastity, or being willing to die for one another, or even healing as they did it — they weren't acts of social co-operation through redistributing resources. They were the work of the kingdom because they marked the alternativeness of an identity which lived out of the future of God, not from the world's potential.

Snarl It's softened your brain. This alternative eschatology stuff! The only alternative society people want is *this* one, with its destructive elements minimised, with injustice eliminated, with the possibilities of creativity maximised, with people able to taste the richness and beauty of the world, comradeship, food, work, music, laughter, the variety of human culture, travel, love, shared joy and sorrow. There *is* no world but this to be human in, and at the moment while you twitter on about an alternative, millions live as sub-human. Poverty, fear, hate, oppression and shame eat them alive. The gospel is that they needn't be eaten. And that is a gospel to be acted, not just spoken.

Swither And death?

Snarl What about it?

Swither Doesn't it eat them?

Snarl Oh, shut up about that: it's just your private obsession. If people have a full and happy life, they don't mind dying so much.

Swither I'd have hoped they'd mind more.

Snarl But we can't do anything about that, and we can do plenty about plenty. There's no point draining constructive energy on things you can't affect.

Swither Ah, you see, that's my real wonder — whether a church of the crucified Christ can assess constructiveness in terms of the manageable. Aren't we most concerned about things we can't give ourselves, like forgiveness, freedom? That's why we only exist in relation to God.

Snarl Are you backtracking to our old friendly God of

the gaps, Swither?

Swither No, because he doesn't belong only in the gaps. He belongs in all you were saying about the richness of life too, but he belongs there crucially because of the empirical organic connection between life and death which he doesn't endorse. He doesn't stand patting our current existence and culture on the back with avuncular approval; what is deadly in it, he hates, so if we pray 'Thy Kingdom Come' we are also inviting our own judgement. That's not a thing to tell others they should be doing. They must discover that for themselves. We can't impose it.

Snarl Why not, if you think the Gospel properly undermines their cultural complacency?

Swither Oh, come on! It's a terrible responsibility to create uncertainty for someone who's grown up feeling absolutely at home in the world — like breaking the news of death to a child before he meets it. We're not inviting them to a picnic, but to a glory which costs crucifixion. Speaking that, even signing it, must be an immense burden to our naturally psychological harmony-loving selves. The burden can only be absent if you distort mission into sending people tractors and teaching them undialectically to be more contented in the earth.

Snarl I think you're really a horrid Gnostic escaped from the second century, negating the beauty of nature, of matter, of this created world.

Swither No, I want to rescue its beauty: but I suspect that, paradoxically, that cannot be done by cherishing it as it is. Our mission is to be an image of it as it isn't. And I think if we did that we'd find the world fascinated and repelled by our strangeness. Whereas now, by trying to earn their well-founded attention, we offer them fulfilment in their terms, and leave them clueless about the kingdom.

Snarl   So it's back to the church choir, and down with Christian Aid, is it?

Swither   Not necessarily. I think almost any specific action can be done for the right or the wrong reasons, and in one context of meaning it becomes one thing, and in another, another. Probably where the church is already, it can't just pull out of established relationships and commitments. But it might try being truthful about its own being in the world, and whether that does really signal or belie the kingdom.

Snarl   So you deny that the kingdom has come, that eschatology can be and is realised in terms of human fulfilment here and now?

Swither   I think so, sadly. It can be hinted at, but not realised.

Snarl   Well, I think we part company here. You seem to me an unhealthy, disintegrating dualist, and to be judged by the same fruitlessness as the most reactionary pietist. You are as sterile as they are for the wretched of the earth, and I know where to go to do something about that.

Swither   Well, go and do it. And on one level all my instincts are to do that too, to give all my energies to feeding and freeing the world from at least its more blatant nightmares of dehumanisation. But I also suspect that if and when I do that, and am contentedly celebrating the fulness of our mutually shared barn, there will still be a gospel of the kingdom which by then will utterly appal me. I keep saying this other negative thing to stop that happening, because I still hear the Gospel as something of wild hope *beyond* my best dreams, not behind them. I must be kept uneasy at my own enlightened utilitarian axioms, or I may stop hearing it at all.

Snarl   Then we must go our own ways. I find that dangerous idealistic nonsense, psychologically sinister and politically disastrous.

Swither   I'm sorry. I thought you must, since I belong to the world too, and think so myself every other Tuesday and Thursday. But now I don't belong straightforwardly, and my mission is, I suppose, to live out of that tension. I can't hear the Gospel any other way, I'm afraid. But I hope you stay around: because I have my doubts, God forgive me. And probably when I don't have them, God forgive me more.

Acknowledgements

Page 10

W H Auden, from "The Dog Beneath The Skin" in *The Penguin Book of Contemporary Verse*, 1962.

Page 11

George Steiner, *After Babel*, Oxford University Press, 1985.

Page 61

Norman MacCaig, *Collected Poems*, Chatto & Windus, 1985.

Page 63

Bertholt Brecht, *The Life of Galileo*, Eyre & Methuen, 1980.

Page 83

Dietrich Bonhoeffer, *Ethics*, SCM Press, 1978.

The front cover illustration is Blake's sketch for a drawing of the Trinity, currently in The British Library.